STRESSAHOLIC

STRESSAHOLIC

5 STEPS TO TRANSFORM YOUR RELATIONSHIP WITH STRESS

HEIDI HANNA

WILEY

Library of Congress Cataloging-in-Publication Data:
Hanna, Heidi, 1974-
  Stressaholic: 5 steps to transform your relationship with stress/Heidi Hanna.
      pages cm
  Includes bibliographical references.
  ISBN 978-1-118-76602-6 (cloth); ISBN 978-1-118-84138-9 (ebk);
ISBN 978-1-118-84135-8 (ebk)
  1. Stress (Psychology) 2. Job stress. 3. Stress management. I. Title.
  BF575.S75H375 2014
  155.9'042—dc23

                                                         2013035596

Printed in the United States of America

10 9 8 7 6 5 4 3 2 1

With deep gratitude to my family, friends, and clients who
continue to inspire and encourage me on this journey.
May we all commit to taking better care of ourselves each day
so we can continue to give our best to one another.

Contents

Foreword

*S*tressaholic is the human owner's manual we have all been waiting for. As she did in her last book, *The SHARP Solution: A Brain-Based Approach for Optimal Performance*, Dr. Heidi Hanna has made it easy for us to understand and implement simple changes to our daily routine that will result in profound changes to our lives. We can all be so much healthier and happier if we take her advice.

There's no denying it: We are all stressed. We naturally crave novel information—but when is enough, enough? Most of us are inundated with more information in one day than someone would have been exposed to throughout their lifetime just a few centuries ago. We must work to evolve into being able to handle all the pressing needs that we face in modern times.

As a result, we tend to easily fall into lifestyle routines in which we experience the same symptoms as in any other addiction. We can avoid drugs, but overindulgence in food is an addiction that requires daily management. Likewise, stress is unavoidable in modern life. We don't all suffer from it; some of us handle it better than others, and some thrive on it. But as Dr. Hanna points out, unless we balance it with rest and repair breaks, we eventually succumb to symptoms and diseases caused by running on the energy we derive from our addiction to stress.

To recharge your phone, you need to plug it in. But to recharge your brain, you need to unplug it. Although this is not the first book to explain how to do so, it may provide the easiest path yet to a more rewarding and energetic life.

You might feel that Dr. Hanna is talking directly to you when reading *Stressaholic*. She identifies the reasons we are as stressed and exhausted as we are. Yet she does not let those reasons become excuses for not taking the time to balance our brain with rest periods.

Dr. Hanna explains how all our biological processes, both body and mind, undergo natural oscillation. She discusses how some of us are stepping on our body's gas and brake pedals at the same time and what we can do about that. She warns us that we have to expend energy to create energy.

This book can save your life. It provides gentle reminders to make the right choices at mealtime; to start today, not tomorrow; and to exercise a little throughout the day. It explains why you are living off the wrong stimulants, both external and internal, and how you can recharge your energy in a positive and productive way.

Dr. Hanna does not let you get away with procrastination. She is compelling and knowledgeable about stress. Throughout the book, she offers pearls of wisdom culled from scientific studies and reliable facts derived from many sources. Her wisdom and advice are easy to understand and incorporate. Undertaking new life rituals can seem daunting, but Dr. Hanna makes them seem easy—because she explains why you need to change these things before she guides you on how to do just that. Her own fears and symptoms have taken her on a quest to learn more. How lucky for us she found the answers and is now, through *Stressaholic*, sharing them enthusiastically yet firmly with us so that we too can make the adjustments to create the life we desire and deserve.

All of us can benefit from this book. In addition to those who are addicted to the stress that is a regular part of work or home life, the five steps detailed herein can be a lifesaver for military service members and veterans—and should be required reading for all who wear this nation's uniforms. Our prolonged wars and the economic uncertainty that affects us all have made posttraumatic stress ubiquitous in America these days. You cannot be too stressed to benefit from this book. In fact, the more stressed you are, the more you need to make *Stressaholic* your personal owner's manual.

Take a deep breath now, turn the page, and begin your step-by-step guided journey to a new, more relaxed, and resilient you.

—Dr. Daniel L. Kirsch
President, The American Institute of Stress

Preface
Monkey Business

It has been said that you don't need much to catch a monkey—simply a container, tied down to something secure, with a hole cut out just large enough for the monkey to slip its hand inside. Place a banana inside the container and wait patiently. When the monkey reaches in to grab the banana, he quickly realizes that he is stuck, because his banana-grasping fist no longer fits through the original hole. All he needs to do to free himself of the trap is let go of the banana. But monkeys cling to the prize and try to force their way out of the trap. They tire themselves out, making them even easier to catch.

Silly monkey, right? After all, the monkey didn't need to be stuck in that trap. But he didn't know better. We humans would never do something like that.

Or would we?

How many times do we cling to the notion that life should be enjoyed as we destroy our health with high-calorie processed food and a sedentary lifestyle? How much can we enjoy life when we are sick—or worse, dead?

How many times must we catch ourselves just before getting into a serious accident as we multitask while driving or even walking because we crave being constantly connected to what else might be going on in the world?

How many stress symptoms, illnesses, or injuries do we need to suffer through before we recognize that our obsession with perfectionism enslaves us to crave more—despite wearing ourselves out to the point of exhaustion?

Learning to let go and creating healthy balance are constant challenges that everyone faces. The good news is that it isn't impossible to find freedom from the traps of life's tests. We simply need to retrain our bodies and brains to be more aware of the severity of unmanaged stress. We do this by learning how to become more flexible with what life throws at us—specifically, by becoming more resilient to the ups and downs and establishing a work-life rhythm that enables us to perform at our best without compromising our health and happiness.

It's a simple process, but that doesn't mean it will be easy. Take a deep breath, and know that if you follow the steps outlined in this book, you will be able to transform your relationship with stress. You'll let go of the traps that seduced you in the past and finally be free to find some branches to swing on.

My Name Is Heidi, and I Am a Stressaholic

I hate to admit it, but I am not naturally a happy person. I'm not an Energizer bunny, and I am certainly not calm amid chaos. I have struggled with anxiety and depression since childhood, and I am hypersensitive to stress and any stimulation. I hate bright lights, loud noises, and loud people. Crowded rooms make me uncomfortable, and I'm claustrophobic. I have a terrible fear of flying and public speaking; yet I make my living traveling as a professional speaker. I'm not a people person and consider myself to be a good wallflower at social events. I am a multitasker and a daydreamer, and like most other people I've met along my travels, I have self-diagnosed attention-deficit/hyperactivity disorder (ADHD).

I am a work in progress. Although I've struggled to deal with my stress addiction at times, I have trained my brain to focus on the positive, creating a more optimistic lens through which to look at life. As a result, I have built a more resilient operating system—body, mind, and spirit—to help me experience and even welcome stress into my life without letting it break me down or burn me out. In the following pages, I share with you what I have learned through my experience as a stress addict, as well as from thousands of my clients who share my affliction. If you think you might be a stress addict, know that you are not alone. Also know that you can find peace from the constant battles to be everywhere at all times and to be everything to everyone. You can finally allow yourself the rest you need to create a healthy pulse for your life.

Introduction
The Crash

Another exhausting day, another sleepless night. As your head crashes onto the pillow (or couch cushion), you can't possibly fathom how someone could be so physically tired and mentally wired at the same time. You begin a conversation with yourself—the same one that took place the night before, and the night before that one, promising that tomorrow will be different. That you will finally get a decent night's sleep, wake up rested, and make better choices for yourself. You'll go to the gym. Start eating better. Take more breaks. Pick up that meditation practice you've been meaning to start. Go to yoga. Drink more water. Stop the coffee habit—well, maybe reduce it a bit.

Suddenly, the thoughts of all the things that need to get done tomorrow start to beat at your busy brain. Chaotic chatter. Mental gymnastics. To-do lists, timelines, *deadlines*—the worry begins to flood your body as your temperature rises, your heartbeat increases, and you feel like someone is sitting on top of your chest. Panic sets in.

Did you turn the lights off? Set the coffeepot to start in the morning? Hear back from your boss about that proposal? Speaking of proposals, don't forget to buy a gift for your cousin's shindig this weekend. Oh crud, did you make those hotel reservations? Don't forget to check in 24 hours early to get your seats. Seats . . . did you RSVP for the networking event tomorrow night? It's last minute; you'd better do that right now.

You get up to turn on the computer, and your already overwhelmed brain is now being stimulated by the notion that there is some critical emergency (you'd hate to piss off the executive director of the networking group, again) while the glare of your computer screen lights it up with neural noise. You try not to read anything while checking your e-mail but can't help glancing at the long list of communications that have arrived since you shut it down only an hour earlier. You convince yourself that if you do a couple of quick e-mails now you'll save yourself time in the morning. Before you know it, the clock strikes 1:00 AM and you realize you won't get those 8 hours you'd promised yourself earlier in the evening. You haven't gotten a minute of shut-eye, and you're already telling yourself you'll start tomorrow night. The cycle continues.

But is it that bad? I mean, you've likely been operating this way for some time now. Although you don't enjoy the hobbies you used to, find it nearly impossible to make quality time for friends and family, and feel drained and distracted all day, you're able to make it work. You've enjoyed plenty of success, and it's not like you have more stress than anyone else these days. So who are you to make taking care of yourself a priority?

Welcome to the human energy crisis—the epidemic of our time. We're running on empty, and the problem is not that we don't know what to do; it's that we don't have the energy to put any of the practices into place. We know we should eat better. We know we should move our body more regularly. We know we should get more sleep, should take more breaks, and would feel better if we had a greater depth of social connections. It's certainly not rocket science. But what I've learned in over a decade of consulting with organizations about health and performance initiatives is that common sense does not mean common practice.

There is not enough time in the day to get it all done. There never will be. This perception of not having enough—whether it be time, money, food, energy, or love—sends a message to the brain that there is a potential emergency. This immediately triggers our innate stress response, which is designed to motivate us to get more of what we need. The problem is, if we never sense that we have enough, we will always be in a state of chronic stress, whether we recognize it or not.

The current human energy crisis is causing us to repeatedly beat up our operating systems. This not only damages our productivity and performance, but it also chips away at our health and happiness. What's worse, the lack of real energy has created a deficit that only seems to be filled by false sources of energy, whether it's coffee and energy drinks to get up or alcohol and sleeping pills to come back down. Like a credit card purchase, we are able to ignore the ever-increasing energy deficit building up at a cellular level in ways such as chronic inflammation, yo-yo metabolism, and cortisol buildup as long as we don't take time to open the bill.

Everything about the human operating system is designed to oscillate—from heartbeats to brain waves to blood sugar fluctuations. Yet most of us live our lives like a flatline. We put the pedal to the metal from the moment our alarm jolts us out of bed, just as we feel like we've finally drifted to sleep. The problem is not only that we're constantly on the go but that our stress response also causes us to have one foot simultaneously on the brake, grinding our gears. The constant perception that we don't have enough— time, money, energy, and so on—prompts the brain to trigger a neurochemical cascade that puts our entire system on high alert 24/7. The results of this are deadly.

Although we know that stress kills (and if you didn't already, you certainly will by the end of this book), we haven't been able to find a solution that works. There are three main reasons for this. First, change, even positive change, requires energy. Although we know stress is bad for us and wastes precious energy resources, trying to change our thoughts and behavioral patterns may cost even more energy. So the brain quickly talks us out of making the effort. If we're already operating in survival mode by conserving energy, the last thing the brain wants to do is spend more energy trying to change what seems to be working.

Second, our lack of energy has made us neurochemically dependent on sources of stress to provide us with the stimulation we need to maneuver through life. Stress is addictive; it acts on the same brain regions as other addictive substances and behaviors, such as sugar, gambling, shopping, and sex. It tells our system that being on high alert is a great idea and something we need to continue to do. We get a rush from stress, craving things that are novel even if they're not necessarily good for us. That rush propels us through the daily grind and can even cause us to wait until the last minute for a greater stress buzz and what we perceive to be improvements in focus and attention.

Finally, programs of the past have looked at ways to manage stress itself—to try to shift the external cause of what ails us. In reality, the only thing we have control over is our relationship with stress. Stress will always be there, and if you think you're stress free, you can be certain that another storm cloud is on its way. That's the nature of life. Stress is not the problem; our response to stress is what robs us of our health, happiness, and potential for success. This is why we must transform our relationship with stress so that we can become more resilient and even use stress for our benefit.

The Stressaholic Recovery Process: Recharge Your Energy, and Then Reprogram Your Life

Two key shifts must happen to break free from stress addiction. First, we need to recalibrate our operating system by replenishing necessary energy at the most basic levels: chemical and cellular. We must then reprogram our lifestyle by rewiring our habits of thought and behavior.

The first three steps of the stressaholic recovery process are designed to help you recharge your energy by (1) eliminating unnecessary stress and stimulation; (2) nourishing the brain and body with energy-enhancing nutrients, such as glucose, oxygen, and positive endorphins; and (3) strengthening neural connections and overall mind-body fitness to increase your available energy supply. This recharge process shifts your system out of deficit-based survival mode and into a more opportunity-based state that is resilient and primed to grow rather than break down from stress.

The final two steps of the stressaholic recovery process help you reprogram your habits, both in how you think and how you act. First, we train your brain to have a healthier, more positive perspective of the world around you, which makes stress more manageable. With adequate energy in the tank and an optimistic mindset, you'll be able to recognize stress as an opportunity for growth rather than a threat to survival. In the final step, we look at ways to establish healthy oscillation in your routines at home and at work, creating the ups and downs that make up your optimal performance pulse and allowing you to be productive, creative, and engaged while getting adequate rest and recovery to stabilize energy. This involves setting boundaries, establishing expectations, using the right attitude, and allocating adequate time to create habits—what I call BEATs. We discuss real-world examples of individuals and organizations that have created BEATs to help them thrive amid chaos.

The stressaholic recovery process is broken into five simple but challenging steps. Together, these steps build your physical, mental, and emotional resilience toward stress, allowing it to build you up instead of breaking you down:

Step 1: Rest: Balance brain chemistry with strategic relaxation and recovery.

Step 2: Repair: Calm and nourish cells with energy-enhancing nutrients.

Step 3: Rebuild: Strengthen mental and physical fitness to optimize energy reserves.

Step 4: Rethink: Shift your perspective to see stress as a challenge instead of a threat.

Step 5: Redesign: Develop BEATs that provide structure for ongoing energy management and oscillation.

Depending on the level of your stress addiction and the amount of time and energy you have available to work your way through the recovery process, this program can be done in three minutes, three days, three weeks, or three months. The more you can invest in optimizing your personal energy management through this program, the greater the results.

At the conclusion of each step of the process is one specific exercise that will be the core of your practice: a simple meditation or visualization that you can read and use in silence or download from my website (www.synergyprograms.com/stressaholic) for a guided experience. These simple techniques help you build a toolbox of practices you can return to repeatedly as you strengthen your resilience through training.

Although we can't often control the external factors that contribute to stress, we can create a stronger, more stress-resilient operating system—body, mind, and spirit. We do this by eliminating excess stress, nourishing with essential and supportive nutrients, and training our brains and bodies with strategic exercises that enable us to function at our best, despite difficult circumstances. Then, we improve our operating system by changing our perspective of stress to one that is more positive and developing rituals and habits that support our new way of life. We can't make stress go away, but we can transform our codependent relationship with it.

Understanding Stress Addiction

Worry is like a rocking chair. It gives you something to do, but it gets you nowhere.

—Erma Bombeck

1

Are You a Stress Addict?

If you're reading this book, chances are (1) you recognize you're a stress addict; (2) you have a concerned friend, family member, or colleague who thinks you're a stress addict; or (3) you are in denial.

Because the experience of stress is different for each individual, it's hard to know for sure whether you have an unhealthy dependence on stress. The following few questions may help you figure it out:

- Do you thrive on tight deadlines?
- Do you often leave things until the last minute?
- Do you have a difficult time doing nothing?
- Does it take you a few days off to feel like you're on vacation?
- Do you spend much of your vacation time thinking about work?
- Do you constantly worry about what you might be missing?
- Do you feel stressed when you're disconnected from your cell phone or computer?
- Do you find it difficult to turn your brain off at night to sleep?
- Do you feel as though there is never enough time to get things done?
- Do you ever feel as though the work you put in for the day is not enough?
- Do you lack time to see your friends or participate in hobbies you used to enjoy?
- Do you feel as though you're constantly running from one thing to the next?
- Do you find yourself finishing, or wanting to finish, other people's statements?
- Do you wish I'd stop asking questions so that you can get on with the book?

Chances are, you answered "yes" to many of these questions. But who cares? We all have stress, and it's not going anywhere—so we might as well accept it, right? I once had a client tell me, "I love my stress and I don't want to manage it." She spoke aloud the truth that so many of us are living, whether we accept it or not: We thrive on stress. It makes us feel driven to succeed, boosts our energy, and gives meaning to our life. Our conversations often seem to involve a competition of who's more stressed. "How are you?" "Stressed." "Me too." Then the parties go on to explain why they're so stressed, with the person who's worse off winning in our backward way of thinking. This twisted social story tells us that the busier we are, the more stressed we are, the more important we are. Take *Seinfeld*'s George Costanza, who made it a point to look annoyed so that his boss would assume he was doing something important.

The problem is not that you can't handle your stress. You're likely doing a fabulous job getting the things done that need to get done, meeting deadlines, and even attending a social event once in a while (especially if it's work related). But what is your experience of your life? Are you taking time to appreciate what you're working so hard to accomplish, or are you merely speeding through to tackle the next item on your to-do list?

Perhaps more important, are you aware of the long-term impact that this stress-filled life has on you? Probably not. Or maybe, like most addicts, you know the consequences of your behavior but are so hooked on it that coming down from stress feels uncomfortable. With such a busy schedule, it's easier to stay amped up than deal with the detox of letting go. Remember the advertisement "This is your brain on drugs"? It made a lasting impression. Unfortunately, it's not just drugs that can cause your brain to feel scrambled. Unmanaged stress might be just as dangerous.

Stress (and drugs) have been shown to have the following side effects: increased heart rate and blood pressure, increased blood sugar, breakdown of muscle tissue, decreased digestive functioning, ulcers, blood clotting, migraines, skin problems, premature aging, loss of brain cells, social isolation and loneliness, anxiety, panic attacks, depression, substance abuse, relationship problems, lack of focus, multitasking, and disengagement. A

20-year study by the University of London completed in the early 1990s found that unmanaged reactions to stress were a more dangerous risk factor for cancer and heart disease than either cigarette smoking or high-cholesterol foods.[1] Stress may even be as addictive as drugs. In addition to the hormones adrenaline and noradrenaline, stress releases the "feel good" chemical dopamine, which encourages repeat behaviors by activating the reward center in our brains. This may be at the heart of many addictive behaviors and substance abuse issues.

Although it may seem a bit extreme to consider stress an addictive substance, just about anything can become addictive depending on the individual who is responding. Addiction expert Stanton Peele has suggested that any habit can become excessive, compulsive, or life endangering. According to Peele, "Addiction . . . is not a label to be applied to specific things but to an involvement a person creates in time or space."[2] It's all about the relationship that we build with our habits of behavior.

When we lose sight of our natural pulse—or worse, intentionally disrupt it to accomplish something—we trigger an adaptive response that becomes addictive. At its core, addiction is a dependence on some external or internal stimulus that causes either a feeling of pleasure or the avoidance of pain. Early-stage stress addiction usually attracts us to sources of stress to get something positive—a neurochemical satisfaction such as dopamine release, an intrinsic (internal) reward such as feeling needed, or an extrinsic (external) benefit such as money, power, or success.

As our addiction progresses, however, it becomes less about what we might get and more about avoiding loss, which brings with it an even stronger tie to our basic survival mechanisms. Instead of intentionally turning to stress-providing stimulation for positive reinforcements, we require them to avoid the pain of its absence. We shift from triggering positive dopamine to avoiding negative cortisol, from seeking importance to avoiding insignificance, and from accomplishing success to merely remaining employed. This fear-based shift moves us from what appeared to be healthy striving to merely surviving.

We can reverse this process by neurochemically rebalancing our brain, nourishing our mind and body with love and support, and establishing training behaviors or habits that strengthen our ability to resist stress's addictive nature. As we've already discovered, stress is not the problem. Depending on or accepting stress without recovery despite hazardous consequences, such as fatigue, dissatisfaction in life, loss of joy, and anxiety, is what destroys our health, energy, and engagement.

Stress is neither good nor bad; it just is. Therefore, it is not the existence of stress that causes an addictive dependence; rather, it's our individual response to the stress in our lives over time. Each person has unique experiences with stress throughout the life span; certain situations cause severe disability, while others enhance learning and facilitate growth.

A life without stress would be stressful. It would push us out of our comfort zone in the opposite direction, with a lack of stimulation for growth. Research shows that one of the highest spikes in human mortality occurs within six months of retirement. It is quite dangerous to go from being always "on" to a screeching halt. The human system is not designed to function in a state of all or nothing, yet because of our hectic environment and constant connection, people tend to be pulled back to the extremes. To operate most effectively, we need to find the balance between stress and recovery that enables us to experience challenge and growth without constantly breaking down.

As discussed in Chapter 3, peak performance in sports, business, and other competitive endeavors occurs at the pinnacle of stress, where there's just enough meaningful, focused stimulation to energize our efforts without going over the top and burning out. The challenge that most people have in finding this balance at the peak is getting pulled into increasingly stressful situations without allowing the necessary rest or recovery time. As a result, the system starts to depend on false sources of energy to push through the symptoms of fatigue until we experience an energy crisis. When that happens, even the harshest stress hormones can't get us up in the morning or through a simple task.

Understanding Stress

Attempting to come up with a universal definition of stress is a lot like trying to define love; it can mean so many different things to different people, and its true experience lies in the eyes of the beholder. The simplest and most helpful definition of stress that I've discovered comes from Hans Selye, a pioneering stress researcher who is often accredited with discovering, or at least first conceptualizing, our modern notion of stress. In 1936, Selye coined the word *stress* as being "the non-specific response of the body to any demand for change"[3] after noticing that laboratory animals who were subjected to acute physical stimuli (such as deafening noise, blaring light, or extreme temperatures) exhibited similar pathological changes, including stomach ulcers, shrinkage of lymphoid tissue, and enlargement of the adrenal glands. He later showed that persistent, chronic stress could cause these animals to develop diseases similar to those seen in humans, such as heart attacks, stroke, kidney disease, and rheumatoid arthritis.

Although the word *stress* quickly became associated with negative threats and responses, Selye also recognized that any definition should also include good stress, or what he called *eustress*. This differentiation between positive eustress and negative distress helped to categorize the initial stimulus. However, it still didn't provide a true separation in how individual responses might differ. Many people have negative stressors that cause growth and a positive outcome, while others experience significant benefit that includes positive stress—and still find themselves suffering negative consequences. As you look back on your life, you can most likely see how the periods when you experienced the most growth were also some of the most challenging. At the same time, you probably know people who despite seeming to "have it all" complain about the minor details of their existence, such as choosing cabinet colors for a new home, or even create drama when it's not there.

Perhaps this conundrum is what caused the idea of stress to revert to a one-size-fits-all concept—describing not just the stimulus but also the experience and the outcome. As one physician explains in a 1951 issue of the *British Medical Journal*, "Stress in addition to being itself, was also the cause of itself, and the result of itself."[4] Stress continues to be difficult to define because it is ultimately grounded in the perception of the individual having the experience. Circumstances such as prior life experiences, sense of control, and current level of resilience can all play a role in determining whether people simply drag themselves along through chronic, overwhelming stress or use the opportunity as a stimulus for personal growth.

We can't control what's already happened to us and are oftentimes dealing with elements beyond our control. However, the critical factor in how we respond to stress is our personal resilience, which can change our response to stress across all levels—body, mind, and spirit.

The Stress Response

Let's first look at our ingrained stress response as we work to create a simple understanding of how stress affects the human operating system. According to stress researcher Robert Sapolsky,[5] all vertebrates respond to stressful situations by releasing hormones such as adrenaline and cortisol to mobilize energy throughout the body, particularly in those areas that allow us to fight our way out of or flee from danger, such as the large muscles in our lower body. Our evolved nature means that humans are the only species able to imagine a potential threat and respond as if it were actually happening in the moment. Regardless of whether the stress we face is real or imagined, the impact on the body and brain is identical.

As a result, physiological changes ensue: an increase in heart rate, blood flow, and available blood sugar to provide fuel for energy production. This enhanced energy metabolism is beneficial in the short term; it leads to increases in strength, improvements in short-term memory, and enhanced immune functioning.

The problem is that we engage the same response even if we are not truly in danger. Over time, the responses that were meant to protect us start to have the opposite effect, causing internal wear and tear on both the body and the brain. This parallels our internal inflammatory response, which is designed to help us repair acute damage but over time begins to attack even healthy cells, causing more harm than good.

Acute (short-term) response	Chronic (long-term) response
Increase in adrenaline	Increase in cortisol
Increase in heart rate	Continued strain on heart and arteries
Increase in blood sugar	Excess sugar stored as fat
Enhanced immune functioning	Increased inflammation
Improved short-term memory	Poor decision making

In addition to the simple but powerful hormonal shifts that occur, stress that persists over time, accumulates to toxic levels, or if not given adequate time for recovery, can speed up the development of life-threatening diseases and disorders. Although stress has not yet been shown to cause any particular illnesses, it has been correlated with all of modern society's major diseases: heart disease, stroke, cancer, diabetes, and dementia. The exact connection between chronic stress and disease is still not clear, but many studies under way may soon provide a better picture.

One new area of research seems to pinpoint the impact of chronic stress on our genetic coding and a particular part of our

DNA molecule called the telomere. A simple way to think of a telomere is that it functions like the cap on the end of shoelace. Telomeres experience normal erosion during cell division, but this aging process may speed up as a result of chronic stress. As the protective coating begins to wear away, it allows the sensitive fabric underneath to become damaged and frayed. Elizabeth Blackburn and her colleagues at the University of California at San Francisco discovered that chronic stress and perception of life stress both affected three biological factors—the length of telomeres, the activity of telomerase, and levels of oxidative stress, all of which speed up the biological aging process. People undergoing the greatest perceived levels of stress were said to have a biological age that was 10 years greater than their chronological age.[6]

Exciting developments in biotechnology will soon enable us to measure both the internal damage we've experienced through unmanaged stress and the changes and improvements we're able to initiate using techniques such as those discussed in Parts 2 and 3 of this book. Until then, it's important that we pay close attention to our symptoms of imbalance, noticing when there are warning signs being sent by our body and brain, such as fatigue, irritability, anxiety, depression, changes in appetite, and illness. If we stay constantly amped up on stress hormones without taking a break from time to time, we may be able to avoid the temporary disruption of warning signs and symptoms but find ourselves running out of steam with a debilitating personal energy crisis.

Overload, Overwhelm, Over It All

Stress is both additive and accumulative, meaning that the number of stressors, the intensity of each, and the frequency and length of time each persists all combine to create the total effect on your system. This is similar to how food affects your digestive system's glucose response. You may have heard of the glycemic index; this is a score that's given to each food to determine how quickly the nutrients break down into usable blood sugar in the body. It was once thought of as a guideline for food selection. However, the glycemic index score alone leaves much to be determined; the way that food is prepared and other foods you eat in combination ultimately impact how you react to the food. What is more important to evaluate is the total glycemic load. This requires calculating many factors that are usually too time consuming to use readily in real-life situations and are often unknown, particularly if you're not the one preparing the foods.

In the same way, it probably doesn't make sense to attempt to calculate your actual stress load at any moment. Yet it is still an important factor to keep in mind when considering how you are dealing with the stresses of life. Stress builds from the inside out, meaning that the irritants and stimulation we experience at a cellular level affect our systemwide resilience. Rather than freaking out about all the minor details going on around you that you can't influence, it's more important to focus on what is under your control: how you manage the critical elements of recovery (energy management) and perception (information management).

If we are not mindful of our stress and recovery balance we can easily find ourselves fighting off fatigue, drawn to even greater amounts of stress in order to feel energized. At the same time, the way we perceive our current stress load often leads to the feeling of being overwhelmed. As a result, we can experience adrenal dysfunction, exhaustion, or burnout. There are some warning signs. If you feel worn down—like you've experienced a dramatic shift in your energy level—or if you have an unusually difficult time recovering from illness or injury, you might find it helpful to meet with a medical practitioner who specializes in adrenal dysfunction.

My personal journey with fatigue felt like I had stepped onto a roller coaster I didn't want to ride, although the outcome for me was positive and led to my desire to write this book. Ultimately I determined that the label used to describe this syndrome, or classification of symptoms, was not necessary in creating my process of healing. In case it's helpful for you, I'd like to share a bit of my experience.

Less than a year ago, I went from running one half marathon per month to barely being able to tolerate a half minute of jogging on the treadmill. I knew I was burning the candle at both ends with my travel and workload, but I had always been able to get myself going when I needed to workout. I felt like my exercise routine was critical in keeping my energy levels adequate (not ideal) and my anxiety levels under control. Despite regularly traveling cross-country and dealing with ever-changing time zones, I pushed myself to get to the gym—even if it meant getting up in the morning at what would have been nonsensical hours at home.

A chance meeting with an integrative medicine doctor opened my eyes to what might have caused my sudden fatigue (although I realize when looking back on it that it didn't come on so suddenly). He pointed out that it might be the symptom of an underlying condition that caused a significant weakening of my adrenal glands or a systemic concern that kept the adrenal process from effectively doing its job. I found myself weeping during a follow-up conversation, when he explained the causes and common symptoms of adrenal dysfunction. I told him that I was terrified that what I had been experiencing was just a mental battle with depression and anxiety or, even worse, that it was the way I was destined to spend my life. I'd grown up hearing that my symptoms were "all in my head," so I assumed someone was going to tell me to get over myself and get on with life. Fortunately, this doctor knew that a core condition was likely causing my symptoms, was convinced that I was quite far along the spectrum of exhaustion, and ordered a few simple tests to see what was going on. Most important, he believed that there was a solution to my problem and that the treatment was something I would be able to facilitate on my own with a little help.

I received the results of my lab work not long after, and sure enough, the doctor identified what appeared to be late stages of burnout. He thoroughly explained to me what happens as a result of early trauma and continued chronic stress on the physiology of the body, in particular the small but powerful glands of the adrenal system. I felt a sense of hope as I decided to follow the treatment protocol for the first few days. Then I started to doubt myself, turning back to the old stories in my head about natural remedies versus medical diagnostics.

So as any good researcher would do, I decided to check in with my regular doctor to make sure there were no underlying conditions causing my severe fatigue. He informed me that the only truly accurate way to determine whether an adrenal disorder existed (notice the shift from dysfunction to disorder) was for me to undergo a blood test that would stimulate my glands to see whether they responded.

The next day, my physician called me on the phone to deliver the "good" results. He stated that there was no indication of any problem with my adrenal glands, and went on to suggest that I focus on the positive—that I was "functional." This was followed by a recommendation to see my shrink.

I'm not saying that my decision to seek medical care was unwarranted or a waste of time. It is always wise to look for underlying medical problems when the body isn't responding the way we know it should. That said, as I'm sure you can imagine, I was not willing to settle for a life of being "functional." I strive to be able to run on a treadmill for more than 30 seconds; I know it can be part of a healthy life. Although I don't need to go back to running a half marathon a month (probably not the best choice when traveling every week and feeling exhausted), the ability to be consistently physically active and feeling energized enough to do my job well are important to me. I'm guessing, because you're still reading this book, that it's important to you as well.

I share my story to let you know that if you're feeling less than optimal, it is up to you to seek the type of care that you need. I don't think recovery from fatigue requires a host of supplements and alternative treatments for most people, but it probably does for some. The information that I provide about recharging your energy will certainly get you on the right path to healing your tired body, mind, and spirit. But if you need additional information, I encourage you to seek a practitioner who is wise to the integrative medicine approach (who does not ignore traditional medicine but rather integrates long-practiced traditions of both the past and the present). In the meantime, let's look at why something we know can be bad for us is so difficult to resist.

What Is Stress Addiction?

The addictive nature of stress affects us at multiple levels of our operating systems—biological, psychological, and social. Any form of addiction derives its strength from the biopsychosocial dependence that's accumulated over time.

Biologically, we have an ingrained response designed to protect us from threats in our environment. Often called the fight-flight-freeze response, these brain-based chemicals are triggered by our perception of stress—whether it's positive or negative and acute (short term) or chronic (long lasting). Depending on the way we interpret the situation, the chemical response in our brain can be quite different, resulting in a unique systemwide stress response. Take, for example, the idea of a challenge versus a threat. Two people in the same scenario may assess their abilities and determine that they either have what they need to get through the experience unharmed or fear they won't rise to the challenge. For example, when people feel supported by others, they estimate the slope of a hill to be less steep than when they stare at the climb alone. The same situation with a different perspective leads to a different experience.

This means that our psychological response, which consists of both our mental and our emotional evaluations, has the power to dictate the physiological response. In this case, how we think drastically changes how we feel.

As part of our assessment of stress, the brain also takes into account our social norms, expectations, and perceived level of support—what we might call our *collective story*. The world today has clear societal messages that can sway our interpretation of circumstances. We are constantly being bombarded, primarily by our 24-hour news media, with the notions that the world is a dangerous place and there is not enough good to go around.

In addition, our constant connection to technology gives our brain a boost of feel-good chemicals each time we anticipate a new message, be it a blessing or a threat. According to a study by Nokia, the average mobile phone user checks his device every 6.5 minutes during the day, or 150 times while he's awake.[7] It's no wonder people have begun to experience what's been called phantom vibration syndrome, where they feel a vibration on the skin near their pocket and go to pull out their phone only to discover it was a false alarm. This can happen when the phone is in a different room, or while the person is watching TV or even is in the shower.

Our brains are hardwired to crave new information. Each time we are exposed to novelty, we experience a release of dopamine, a chemical associated with the brain's reward center. This affinity for all things new may also be at the root of our multitasking addiction; we are always a bit curious about what else might be going on when we're trying to focus on a single task. With access to so much information, it's easy to find a distraction these days.

Whether stress should be considered addictive continues to be a hot topic—and a fun debate. Yet it's clear that certain factors keep us connected to stress as an energy provider—especially when we aren't managing our energy effectively through more lasting sources, such as healthy nutrition, physical activity, relaxation, adequate sleep, and strong social connections. If you look at the medical model of addiction, it seems clear that stress can be used as a drug of choice just like any other mood-altering substance or behavior. According to the *Diagnostic and Statistical Manual of Mental Disorders*,[8] for something to be classified as an addiction, it should meet the following requirements. As you read through them, ask yourself whether any sound familiar when it comes to stress or stimulation in your life.

1. The impact of the substance is decreased with repeated use, requiring greater amounts to sustain the desired effect (tolerance). (In other words, you need more stress to get the same "high.")
2. Withdrawal symptoms (such as irritability, headaches, fatigue, depression, anxiety, or other physical or psychological changes) experienced when substance is not in use, or the substance is taken in order to avoid symptoms of withdrawal.
3. Continued use over a longer period of time or in greater amounts than originally intended. (You experience high levels of stress to meet a deadline, tell yourself you'll take time off once the task is completed, but find yourself quickly slipping back into stress mode for the next thing.)
4. Desire to stop or unsuccessful efforts to cut down or control substance use. (You know you should take breaks, but can't seem to make them a priority.)
5. Significant time spent obtaining substance or recovering from its use.
6. Decreased participation in important social, recreational, or work-related activities due to substance use. (You skip out on meeting up with friends or taking much-needed decompression time to stay connected to work and amped up on stress.)
7. Continued use despite physical or psychological consequences either caused or made worse by the substance. (You see the consequences of unrelenting stress in your life, but continue to attempt to push past the pain or discomfort.)

Nature versus Nurture

During my research process, I also became aware of a hypersensitization that some people experience with regard to stress.

Essentially, a trauma or series of traumas overstimulates the human stress response for a certain period, making it less effective at managing future episodes. Studies have evaluated individuals who have experienced childhood trauma such as physical or sexual abuse and found that the greater the early stress, the more damaging the exposure to stress later in life.[9] This may be part of the reason some people seem prone to worry, whereas others roll with the punches. There is a genetic component to our patterns of thought and behavior, and many people who exhibit type-A personalities were born that way. However, we know that even genetic predispositions aren't a guaranteed fate. We're increasingly seeing that while genes "load the gun," it's lifestyle that "pulls the trigger."

You can compare this to people who seem genetically wired to develop type 2 diabetes. Although they may be more sensitive to insulin swings and imbalances, their lifestyle choices mostly determine whether they end up becoming insulin resistant and developing the disorder. In the same way, repeatedly experiencing situations that we perceive to be stressful may "wear out" the body's ability to cope. Over time, we may either become overly sensitive or lack sensitivity in that department. With continued exposure, the body's natural biological mechanisms weaken or even begin to fight themselves.

However, we can reduce or even remove painful symptoms by bringing the body back into balance through a process of resting, repairing, and rebuilding—and by undergoing what I refer to as the "recharge process."

I can clearly identify scenarios in my life that led to my hypersensitization to stress. I've been aware of these for decades yet still struggled to rebalance my system to be less out of sync. I'm sure you've been through similar situations. We can recognize where the problem started, but mere knowledge of the cause does not provide us with a solution. The key to recovery is to first acknowledge and understand the underlying cause of the sensitivity and then work smarter (not harder) to repair the damage and build resilience to stress moving forward.

From One Addict to Another

I know all of this not just through research but because it is my story too. After pushing for years, using excess stress and survival-based emotions to help me cope with feeling I was in over my head, my brain and body finally stopped me in my tracks. I feel fortunate that it wasn't a more severe message, and I remind myself every day that I have been warned. But it was enough to show me that the way I was working wasn't working.

I was diagnosed at an early age with an anxiety disorder and therefore knew stress would always be part of my life. I was also clear on what I wouldn't be able to tolerate, including stressful situations such as flying and public speaking. When my former boss first hired me for the Human Performance Institute in Orlando, Florida, I remember him beaming with excitement when he told me that with time and experience I'd have the opportunity to travel and become a keynote speaker. I quickly informed him that I was interested in the job but only if I could stay at home and train the groups that came to our facility to limit my time on the road. I was thrilled that my lack of excitement about the "adventure" of being a road warrior didn't cost me the job.

Two years later, after being pestered by a client, I agreed to travel a short distance to give a keynote presentation. What happened next changed my life. My head was spinning with stress during the weeks leading up to the meeting, but about halfway through the session, the audience roared with laughter at something that I said (a good thing, in this case)—and I was hooked. I couldn't believe the attendees enjoyed my talk, and the lineup after the meeting was filled with individuals eager to swap stories and share their gratitude with me.

The ability to connect with people on this deeper level about things that I knew would have a positive impact on their lives was amazing. I quickly recognized that I was being given an opportunity to do work I was truly passionate about, and I couldn't slam the door shut without at least giving it my best try. So I proceeded to work diligently with my client to put together a customized program that ended up giving me opportunities to travel and speak around the globe.

The following year I traveled more than 300,000 miles, visiting places as distant as Hong Kong, Australia, and Greece. I'll never forget the feeling I had stepping off a transcontinental plane; fetching transportation, unsure of currencies or communications; and pinching myself that I was taking this on. Each destination was a new obstacle, each presentation terrified me night after sleepless night, but I kept going—that is, until I couldn't.

With a compromised immune system and constant overwhelming stress I could virtually feel rushing through my veins, my system finally crashed. I had experienced panic attacks as a child, but usually they were fairly quick and mostly harmless. This time the panic seemed to accumulate over a period of days that turned into weeks, and I found myself in the hospital multiple times.

I couldn't shake the feeling of terror, that something had snapped and I would never be able to get on a plane or a stage again. My life as I knew it was over, and for the first time in several years on the road, I called in sick. As I slowly worked myself out of panic mode and into survival mode, I recognized that something had to change. I knew that I needed to take better care of myself to keep from breaking down this way in the future. My first step was to get a massage.

At the time, I simply assumed that massage was something you did when you went to a spa and felt like spending a fortune on being pampered. However, I quickly realized that it was also a way for me to show myself love and support while decreasing the dangerous cortisol hormones that flooded my system. Many years later, I still commit to getting a massage once a week as part of my maintenance plan. We all experience recovery and relaxation differently, so massage might not be the answer for everyone. But I find I'm paying for time to be taken care of—time for me to focus on relaxing my body and quieting my mind. It's not only paid off in terms of health benefits; I have done most of my best work during massage sessions. I've found that the pathways in my brain begin to relax and make new connections, triggering creative thoughts and insight.

I can look back on each personal energy crisis in my life and see clearly how my energy management routine had failed. When I don't "put my oxygen mask on first," my sensitive brain and body let me know immediately. I used to call it a curse; I felt like my brain was somehow broken or I was a freak of nature. But now I consider it a blessing. Most people can push through the fatigue and the exhaustion and can even burn out before realizing something has to be done. They can slowly disengage from things enough to keep their sanity, even if they're regularly disappointed in their lack of energy or engagement. But the longer we push through the pain, the more we inflict internal wear and tear on our system. The sooner we are forced to take a hard look at our stress response, the sooner we can minimize the damage and start to rest, repair, and recharge our bodies and minds.

My name is Heidi, and I'm a stressaholic. Not only have I been put in situations that terrified me, I have put up with them because of the great reward I received for pushing through the pain. What's worse, I miss the stress when it subsides; I crave it so much that I've even re-created it without reason. During the majority of the last decade I spent on the road as a speaker and consultant, I've tried to build in relaxation practices, but I found them boring and quite honestly a "waste of time." Who can meditate when there is so much work to be done and so little time in which to do it? But my stress addiction has taught me that I tell myself stories to support my need for speed. We all do. We've all been fooled by the story that the busier we are and the more stressed we are, the more important we must be. I recall driving to an appointment, glancing down at my phone to check e-mail (something I never do anymore), and feeling depressed staring at an empty inbox because my sense of worth had become wrapped up in how much work I had to do.

The truth is that we can be busy without being stressed and we can have challenges without being worried or anxious. We can take control of our operating system and transform the lens through which we see life to one that is more optimistic and resilient. We can rewire the way our brain perceives stress and experience significant growth as a result—rather than enduring yet another energy crisis. But to do so, we need to design a more optimal way of operating that enables us to take on the stress of life in manageable amounts, with built-in periods of rest and recovery. By creating a more resilient system, we build up our tolerance to stress so that when the most difficult circumstances occur, we can experience our most profound growth as a result.

Many people assume that having more of whatever they need or want—whether it's time, money, power, or the like—will make them happy. But positive psychology research has shown the opposite can be true. Studies of lottery winners discovered that people feel happier up to a certain amount of winnings, most likely due to an increase in security. But along with the positive bolt of benefits comes more challenges: tax payments, greater lifestyle expenses, expectations, family members they didn't know existed, and so on. However, people who have experienced debilitating injuries, such as amputees, face tremendous loss but often rebound with a greater sense of purpose as they rebuild their system and reframe their life. It's not life's circumstances that make the biggest difference in our happiness and well-being; it's our perception of what's going on around us and our ability to cope with, and even learn to embrace, all that it has to offer.

Later in this book I discuss specific rules and mantras that I found helpful in my journey away from stress addiction—such as recognizing I am not my thoughts, realizing recovery is not optional, and finally understanding that taking care of myself is not selfish. I hope that these ideas will help you as you break free from the grasp of stress in your life and move from exhaustion to enlightenment.

2

Why Taking It Easy Is Hard

Have you ever noticed how difficult it is to relax? For something that's supposed to be enjoyable, slowing down can actually cause a great deal of discomfort to someone who's used to being on the go all the time. Try it now. Close your eyes for a few moments, and try to completely relax your body and quiet your mind. See how long it takes for your brain to start wandering to your ever-expanding to-do list or other worries of the day.

Without practice, taking it easy is hard work. We've spent a long time training our brains and bodies to become accustomed to consistent surges of stress hormones, such as adrenaline and cortisol; they provide us with fuel to get things done throughout the day. When we attempt to slow down and let go of our concerns, we can feel mild to moderate depression. We lose stimulation, which triggers an underlying fear that we won't have the energy we need to get things done—again boosting stress hormones in response. This creates a vicious cycle: We start to worry about not worrying, and suddenly we're relieved to be worrying—ah, that feels better.

Although we recognize that chronic stress can be hazardous to our health—even with the best intentions and the necessary knowledge to resolve it—we can find it nearly impossible to let go. Our codependent relationship with stress is just one example of a scenario in which knowing what to do and doing it are two very different things. We therefore need more than just the answers to create lasting behavior change; we need to be able to incorporate those answers into our lifestyle in a sustainable way. All of which requires energy.

Most of us do a terrible job of balancing our energy management budget. As I described in my book *The SHARP Solution: A Brain-Based Approach for Optimal Performance*, your brain acts as the conductor of your energy. Like the chief financial officer (CFO) of an organization, your brain keeps a steady watch on your energy balance to make sure you have the capacity you need to meet survival demands. At the most basic level, this means keeping an adequate supply of glucose (blood sugar) and oxygen distributed regularly to the cells for energy production. In times of a shortage, the brain triggers a cascade of physiological responses to conserve energy throughout the body, fueling only the most critical functions, such as your heart and lungs. When energy levels are low, it becomes difficult to convince the conservative brain that excess expenditures like being patient, loving, and kind are important amid the chaos.

The more we use up our energy throughout the day without refueling, the more our mindset becomes stuck on a perspective of inadequacy or deficiency. Add to that the feeling that we never have enough time to get things done, and we further incite our protective mechanisms. Nothing is more stressful to the human brain than the fear of running out of resources. The mere potential of this occurrence increases stress levels, thereby demanding even more energy from an already depleted system. That's when we can find ourselves physically tired but mentally wired as our bodies attempt to compensate by revving up our stress response.

This push-pull relationship between what we want to do (our heart) and what we need to do (our brain) is why I have come to consider my brain my frenemy. Although it has the potential to fuel my growth and success in challenging times, if I'm not treating it right, it quickly shows me who's boss.

Your CFO Brain versus Your CEO Heart

Depending on how you treat it, your brain can be your best friend or your worst enemy. It can lead you swiftly to your most precious goals and aspirations, or it can derail your journey.

I used an analogy in my last book that bears repeating here, because it paints a clear and helpful picture as to why it can be so difficult to do the things we know we should do. When it comes to our energy management and decision making, there are two leaders of our human operating system. As mentioned previously, the brain acts like a CFO, responsible for managing our most valuable resources. The heart, which keeps us connected to what's most important to us and steers us toward our most critical missions in life, is like our chief executive officer (CEO).

Throughout the day, the brain receives chemical messages from different parts of the body that provide consistent updates on our current energy status. Do we have enough glucose and oxygen to fuel energy production? Are we consuming enough water to keep our cells hydrated? Does our heart feel enough purpose to inspire our spirit? Do we perceive that we have the support of those around us should things take a turn for the worse? If we're running on all cylinders and strategically managing our energy, the brain can allocate resources to make choices and even create new habits of both thought and behavior. However, if we're running low on energy or trying to get by on fumes, the brain quickly switches into conservation mode, fueling only the most essential functions, such as heartbeat and breathing. We should be grateful to our conservative CFO brain, because that type of diligence is the reason that our ancestors were able to survive in times of famine. But when we've come to the end of a long day and we're trying to choose between a healthy salad and a calorie-rich cheeseburger for dinner, our CFO brain usually overrides our CEO heart's desire to eat a more balanced diet.

This means that even though we want to do something, or believe we should do something, our brain often talks us out of it. Exercise is a perfect example of this. When we're exhausted and worn out from the day's demands on our energy, we may think or even believe that we should exercise. But all our CFO brain perceives is another demand for energy—something that we don't have to spend at the moment.

Quickly, a thought pops into mind that we'll start again tomorrow when we have more energy in the tank. This is what makes the brain such a genius: It is the master of convincing us to believe something different from what our heart may feel. If we ask for more energy than we have at the moment, the brain provides a million reasons why it's not a good idea: "We've tried this before and it didn't work," "We're too tired," "It's better for us to rest," or my all-time favorite, "We'll just start tomorrow."

I'll never forget sitting in a hotel lounge as a woman was getting a piece of pie. She turned to the guy next to her and said, "I'm doing Weight Watchers, and I'm counting points. But I'll just start tomorrow." Although her CEO heart may have felt that she wanted to lose weight and eat better to support her goals, her CFO brain was exhausted and needed energy to continue to function optimally. It was tired of the energy roller coaster of the daily grind and even wanted to store extra energy for the future. The brain's default move during an energy shortage is to invest in the storage tanks we call our fat cells—which is one reason our waistlines continue to expand when we're stressed. Few foods make a better investment than a nice slice of pie, especially right before bed.

How can you hope to alter this? The key to sustainable behavior change is to align the CFO brain's *attention* with the CEO heart's *intention*, both of which require energy. It can be helpful to keep this analogy in mind when you're struggling to make good choices. Look at how you've been treating your brain lately and the level of available energy it has before you start beating yourself up. Thank your brain for being so protective of your relationship, and then start showing it a bit more respect.

Running on Empty

The human operating system requires energy 24/7 just to sustain life. To make sure we have enough of what we need, our bodies and brains are hardwired to protect energy reserves when there is a threat of running out. But despite the fact that energy is our most valuable resource, most people fail to manage it effectively. In an effort to get more done in less time, we take shortcuts in fueling our own energy requirements. We eat foods that contain too much of what's bad for us and not enough of what we need.

We sit for long periods throughout the day or overtrain at the gym when we finally get there. We elevate our stress levels so high during the day that we can't wind down at the end of it. We have hundreds of friends on social media but lack time for meaningful face-to-face conversations. As a result, we are running on empty, feeding on fumes with one foot planted firmly on the gas while the other is stuck on the brakes.

In the book's Introduction, I described the common perception that we don't have enough of something, such as energy or time, and how this triggers the stress response that motivates us to get more of it. Because this potential deficit threatens our survival, it instantly puts the brain into a fear-based state. What makes this especially difficult in today's society is that we have access to more information than we could ever obtain in our lifetime. There is always more we could be doing, reading, studying, learning, or knowing. Because our brain is hardwired to crave novel information, whether good or bad, we've become obsessed with obtaining more. We're constantly keeping a bit of our brainpower ready in case we get the chance to learn something new. This mental multitasking keeps us scatterbrained and destroys our ability to engage in the moment.

This phenomenon has become so commonplace in our busy, connected lives that a new acronym conceptualizes this fear of missing out: FOMO. With the boom in social media sites such as Twitter and Facebook giving us constant access to what everyone else is doing at any given time, it's easy to see and compare our circumstances to those of our friends or acquaintances. In the past we compared ourselves to the supermodels in magazines and the glamorous lifestyles of the rich and famous on TV, but now even the girl next door seems to have a more exciting life than we do. I find it ironic that no matter what wonderful things may be happening in my own life, the grass seems just a bit greener on every other side.

One of the greatest costs of the human energy crisis when it comes to organizations is *presenteeism*—when employees show up physically but are not fully engaged mentally or emotionally. Although most people feel they have no choice but to multitask throughout the day because of an overwhelming to-do list, the brain is only able to focus on one thing at a time. When we think we're maximizing productivity by doing multiple tasks at once, we're instead waste precious time and energy while increasing focus-blocking cortisol levels in the brain. Our brains are not designed to multitask; from a survival perspective, the only time we must pay attention to many different stimuli is amid a threat in our environment. It's only natural that our brain doing mental flip-flops compels us to boost energy-enhancing stress hormones to help us deal with the emergency. As we discussed earlier, this is fine when it's a short-term problem but deadly when it's an ongoing saga.

As if killing brain cells were not bad enough, multitasking decreases our performance on the tasks we're juggling and wastes the time we're trying so hard to save. Studies have reported that our productivity decreases by up to 40 percent when we try to do simultaneous tasks.[1] The decrease in our available brainpower is equal to missing out on a full night's sleep and is twice that of smoking marijuana. According to the National Safety Council, using a cell phone, even with a hands-free device, decreases focus on the road by 37 percent.[2]

We think we're saving time, but we're actually spending it with reckless abandonment. Time management experts have estimated that it can take up to 20 minutes to recover from a distraction, with more complex tasks taking a greater toll on what's called *switch cost*—the time taken to adjust mental settings and competition due to carrying over mental controls from the previous task.[3] Simply put, this involves trying to forget the specifics about what we were working on and figuring out how to move on to the next thing. The consequences can be deadly when we're trying to avoid a swerving car on the road. Although not nearly as dramatic, when we're talking to friends while washing dishes or folding laundry, our multitasking brain can pull us away from a meaningful conversation, causing us to misinterpret messages and make important, potentially damaging mistakes.

The harsh reality is that we chronically destroy productivity, waste time and energy, and kill brain cells when we multitask. We also communicate an important message to the brain that there is not enough time to get things done, triggering the stress response and its cascading effects. If we never feel like we have enough, we are always caught up in the vicious cycle of stress addiction. To change this habitual pattern, we must ensure a strategic energy management plan provides our brain and body fuel for survival while rewiring our thought process to perceive a state of abundance rather than one of deprivation. One of my favorite mantras, which we discuss further at the end of Chapter 4, is "I have enough, I am enough," reminding my brain that in this moment all is well.

Brain Drain: Too Much, Not Enough

Stress isn't always caused by not having enough time, money, food, energy, love, and so on. In some cases, it may be triggered by having too much. Unfortunately, modern society seems to promote an all or nothing approach to life; we're either on a diet or bingeing on whatever food we feel like, sticking to an exercise routine or laying on the couch, practicing meditation or going nonstop. We are seldom able to follow the rule of all things in moderation, because moderation is difficult to sustain. It's not exciting, it doesn't stimulate us, and it isn't new. It's boring. In contrast, being all-in feels inspiring and motivating, especially at the beginning, whereas being all-out feels normal and comfortable. We spend a lot of time and energy yo-yoing between what's good for us and what's not good for us, shifting from stimulating change to coasting along.

In addition to wasting resources as we figure out the perfect way to live a healthy lifestyle or simply throwing in the towel, our brain is constantly buzzing with mental chatter. We have about

60,000 to 80,000 thoughts daily, and each thought requires energy, so it's no wonder we feel wiped out at the end of the day. To make things worse, our lack of focus and our chaotic environment create constant distractions that cause us to do mental jumping jacks, thereby wasting even more time and energy.

Our obsession with and access to information destroys our ability and sometimes even our desire to engage in the moment. There is always something else that we think we need to know about or more we could or should be doing. The busier the environment, the more primed we are to be distracted by what else might need our attention. We also can't forget about all the people in our digital social world who may need to know about what we are or might be doing. Tweeting about being here takes me away, and I can no longer fully engage in my experience. Recording video to post on YouTube gives me a narrowed perspective of what's happening and takes me away from my present enjoyment, replacing it with the hope that I'll enjoy it more by being able to share it in the future. We are overly connected yet disconnected. Technology is fabulous when we use it to engage in life but not when we allow it to interfere with it.

Everything that has life has a pulse, a natural rhythm of arising and subsiding, ebb and flow, effort and ease. When we are aligned with our natural oscillation or pulse, we experience more with less effort. In this rhythm, we can enter into a state of flow. But when we fight against ourselves or attempt to push past the resistance we feel, we struggle and mindlessly waste time and energy resources. We must find the balance between effort and ease that enables us to reach our goals without wearing out our reserves. This allows us to push less while achieving more.

Our Serious Stress Problem

We have a love-hate relationship with stress. The media continue to bombard us with the message that we're in an epidemic (started in the 1980s and only getting worse) and that stress is killing us. Clearly, what happens as a result of that harsh warning is more stress. We are stressed about stress, but honestly, we wouldn't have it any other way. If we let it go, we lose the adrenaline rush we've become so dependent on to get through the daily grind. Our brain is wired to help us to do more and be more as a means of securing our survival, so doing nothing feels bad—and as far as the brain is concerned, it's best to keep things the way they are.

As a result of our failed attempts to manage energy, we critically depend on sources of stress to provide us with that false sense of fuel. Similar to the caffeine rush so many of us rely on to wake up and keeping going, our brain becomes amped up on this counterfeit energy. It continues as though there is no problem, while our bodies take a severe beating at a cellular level. This is not just a result of the day-to-day stress of our lives that develops from work, kids, bills, and to-do lists; it also involves the lifestyle choices we make. The foods we eat or don't eat, the sleep we get or don't get, the exercise we do too much or not enough of—all of these things stress our system by knocking us off balance.

As we've discussed, our ingrained stress response acts on the same triggers in the brain as do other addictive substances and behaviors, such as drugs, alcohol, sugar, shopping, gambling, and even falling in love. Our reward system, fueled primarily by a chemical in the brain called dopamine, compels us to keep doing things that we perceive to be helpful for our survival, which includes staying hyperaware of potential threats in our environment during times of stress.

When we repeat a behavior over and over again—such as driving the same route to work each morning—the repetition builds a habit. Add dopamine and the neural connections become even stronger, making it almost impossible to stop even the behaviors that we know are bad for us.

We all know that the substances and behaviors listed earlier are toxic when used in excess. But when the body and brain get a hit of these addictive chemicals, they don't just experience the initial reward response; they also begin to crave it once it's gone. As with any other addiction, our tolerance level increases over time, even when it comes to stress. This means that we need greater amounts of stimulation to get the same endorphin rush, which creates a dependence that makes it increasingly uncomfortable to eliminate sources of stress.

You may consider it a strong statement to call stress an addiction; however, think about how long it takes you to relax when you're on vacation. Or how challenging it is to keep away from e-mail during the day even though you know it's a distraction from other things you may need to focus on. Each phone call, e-mail, or text initiates the reward system in anticipation of something new and potentially positive. Even though we may not enjoy what we hear on the other side, we crave novelty at a neurochemical level.

Our habits aren't necessarily addiction worthy unless they cause negative consequences, persist despite multiple attempts to quit, or both. According to the American Society of Addiction Medicine, "Addiction is a primary, chronic disease of brain reward, motivation, memory and related circuitry. Dysfunction in these circuits leads to characteristic biological, psychological, social and spiritual manifestations. This is reflected in an individual pathologically pursuing reward and/or relief by substance use and other behaviors. Addiction is characterized by inability to consistently abstain, impairment in behavioral control, craving, diminished recognition of significant problems with one's behaviors and interpersonal relationships, and a dysfunctional emotional response. Like other chronic diseases, addiction often involves cycles of relapse and remission. Without treatment or engagement in recovery activities, addiction is progressive and can result in disability or premature death."[4]

The question then becomes, Is stress a problem for you? Ask yourself, Do I feel uncomfortable when I don't have sources of stress keeping me energized to perform? Do I wait until the last minute to get things done? Has stress caused tension or problems in my important relationships? And maybe most important, Do I find it difficult to abstain from stress, feeling cravings to reengage when I know it's more than I am able to handle in the moment?

I can tell you as a stress researcher that the evidence is clear: Without treatment or engagement in recovery activities, stress addiction is progressive and can result in disability or premature death.

Scary Stress Stats

It's important to be aware of how serious our stress problem has become, but please don't stress over the following information. Take a breath, and remind yourself that you're already on the path to getting your stress under control and using it for your benefit instead of letting it break you down.

That said, here is what we are doing to ourselves if we don't take charge of our addiction to stress:

- In 2003, improperly managed stress alone was estimated to have cost U.S. businesses $300 billion each year. Imagine what that number has grown to over the decade.[5]
- U.S. medical experts estimate that 75 to 90 percent of doctor visits are stress related.[6]
- In the United States, 40 million adults suffer from anxiety.[7]
- Mood disorders are estimated to cost more than $50 billion per year in lost productivity.[8]
- Forget the American Dream: 73 percent of American workers say they would *not* want their boss's job.[9]
- Among American workers, 35 percent say their jobs are harming their physical or emotional health, and 42 percent claim that job pressures interfere with their personal relationships.[10]

- American workers also report the following: 62 percent routinely find that they end the day with work-related neck pain, 44 percent reported eyestrain, 38 percent complained of hurting hands, and 34 percent reported difficulty in sleeping because they were too stressed.[11]

- More than half of American employees said they often spend 12-hour days on work-related duties, and an equal number frequently skip lunch because of job demands.[12]

- According to a study by AOL, Americans seem to be addicted to e-mail. Of those surveyed, 59 percent of people who own a portable device, like an iPhone or BlackBerry, check e-mail in bed while in their pajamas; 37 percent check it while they drive; and 12 percent admit to checking e-mail in church. Eighty-three percent of e-mail users admit to checking their mail once a day while on vacation.[13]

Stress continues to be a problem for both our health and our performance, yet it is a difficult topic to discuss because people feel helpless about the stress in their lives, don't want to be considered weak by others because of an inability to cope, or think they thrive on stress and would otherwise lose their competitive edge. Although it's true that some stress can fuel optimal performance, we can't continue to go without giving our system a break. As time goes on, studies like those cited earlier will continue to rapidly surface, providing even more evidence that the way we're working is not working. My hope is that you will take personal responsibility to create a more positive relationship with the stress in your life and that as your family, friends, and coworkers see your progress, they will join you in the journey.

3

How to Use Stress for Success

As you've heard me say time and time again, stress is neither good nor bad; it just is. What determines the impact of stress on our system is our ability to adapt to it. When we are running on empty and operating in survival mode, we become rigid and default to the automated habits that have served us for so long. You'll recall from the prior chapter why the brain considers this the best approach: Any change in habits, even positive, requires an energy investment. When there is nothing in the bank account, the brain has no option but to resort to curbing noncritical spending.

Like an old rubber band, we crack and break down when force is applied to our weakened systems because we lack flexibility. But when we have the energy to be pliable and resilient, we are able not only to bounce back from challenges but also to strengthen our system as a result of the exercise.

Therefore, successful and sustainable stress management must start with a core foundation of energy to keep the brain and body functioning in a more optimal state. This allows the brain to facilitate opportunity-based processes for focus, attention, creativity, flexibility, and endurance over time. The messages that the body's various hormones send the brain to regulate energy flow, and maintain resources like glucose and oxygen, provide the stability we need for optimal functioning.

Consider the stress management strategies in this book— rest, repair, rebuild, rethink, and redesign—as building blocks of a pyramid (see Figure 3.1). The foundational techniques will be those we continue to go back to when we feel overwhelmed or out of balance.

The fundamental strategy of oscillation will serve as the supporting structure we need to continue moving up to the pinnacle of health, happiness, and performance. Once we have adequate rest and recovery built into our routine, we can then look to nourishing nutrients that will strengthen our core practice and provide even more resilience and stability. By using our repair techniques, we will create healthier cells and stronger

FIGURE 3.1

neural pathways in the brain to keep the body and mind performing at their best. We will rebuild these chemical and cellular processes in our final recharge step by incorporating strategic training challenges that temporarily break down our system, a bit at a time, to stimulate just enough stress to cause our system to adapt and become even stronger. It's important to always be cognizant of the rest and repair techniques we need to continue so that the challenges we seek provide an opportunity for growth rather than cause us to break down without building back up.

In the final two steps of the stress management process, we will build upon our foundation of strategic energy management to create a more positive mindset—one that will allow us to perceive the stress in our life as healthy and beneficial. As we rethink stress, we'll be able to use it to our advantage. We'll then continue to create support for our habits of thought and behavior as we redesign our routine to establish an optimal performance pulse: periods of stress balanced with periods of recovery.

Manage Energy by Minding the Gaps

The first step in optimizing the operating system is making sure we have consistent energy throughout the day. The most basic lifestyle choices—eating every 3 to 4 hours, moving at least every 90 minutes, staying hydrated, getting adequate sleep, and maintaining solid relationships—all help the brain and body to obtain the fuel they need. Although these might seem simple, running our systems off stress hormones can easily fool us into thinking that we have all the energy we need in the moment.

If you were stranded on a deserted island and truly in danger (which is how the brain perceives any real or imagined threat to your system), the last thing you'd want to do is take time to grab a snack, go for a leisurely stroll, or take a quick snooze. The ability to temporarily ignore signals such as hunger, thirst, or even fatigue is built into the stress response. This is why we lose our appetite and feel like we can go days without eating the moment we experience a significant stressor. Think about getting bad news at work or finding out a deadline was suddenly expedited. The last thing we need is to feel distracted by stomach growls when there is critical work to be done. So why do we overdo it when we finally sit down for a meal at the end of the day? If stress persists or is chronic, the brain eventually wants to compensate for the energy deficit. This is why it seems to take forever to feel satiated once we open a bag of potato chips or crack a cold beer.

Unfortunately, we cannot always rely on our natural body signals to tell us what we need when we're dealing with overwhelming stress. We must therefore create energy-enhancing rituals that prompt us to return balance to our system, regardless of how we might be feeling in the moment. In Part 2 of this book, I explain a simple process to start to recharge your energy, first providing rest at a chemical and cellular level, then nourishing your system with essential nutrients, and finally generating even more energy reserves through strategic training that isn't tiring or overwhelming. It helps you switch out of survival mode and enables your body and brain to function more optimally, even in the midst of stress.

Remember, everything about the human operating system is designed to oscillate, from brain waves to heartbeats, blood sugar levels, and inhalations and exhalations. Yet most people get up in the morning and go all day without taking a moment to pause and reset. We all know that a flatline is bad news when we're measuring biological processes, but because most people can't get a clear picture of their energy throughout the day, they are unaware of how problematic this can be. When we override our natural rhythms, we must rely on temporary sources of energy such as external stimulants, like coffee and energy drinks, or internal stimulants, like adrenaline and cortisol. Although this may be fine in acute situations, repeated reliance creates additional wear and tear on an already aging biological clock.

One of the most critical elements of energy management is building in time and creating space to reestablish our natural rhythms, or what I call our *energetic pulse*. There are many ways to do this, and I describe more specifically how to create a unique pulse in the last step of the stressaholic recovery process in Chapter 8. The key is to take time to develop a routine that allows adequate recovery for the amount of stress we're experiencing. The more stress we have, the more recovery we need.

I learned this fairly early in my career, because I experienced the worst dips in my physical and emotional energy right after speaking engagements. Thankfully, my parents started to notice this during my conversations with them and would offer support as I started to whine to them about my energy crash. As I became more aware of my energetic cycles, I quickly noticed that the more chaotic my work experience (more planes, trains, and automobiles usually did the trick), the more exhausted I felt.

However, it wasn't just the travel, jet lag, and restless nights. Once I was managing my energy more effectively, I still noticed a pattern: The higher my energy while performing on stage, the lower I dropped afterward. Trying to fight it only made things worse. I would get so aggravated and anxious about my fatigue that I would push myself through challenging workouts and beat myself up to "just be happy," but nothing worked. This continued until I realized that I was on a roller coaster: Even taking care of myself the way I should wasn't going to prevent occasionally dips.

I'm not a roller coaster fan, but I wanted to continue to do the work I feel so passionate about. I was willing to plan and prepare myself for the resulting drop in energy by scheduling accordingly and making sure to reach out for support as needed. Although I haven't yet mastered the Heidi Hanna roller coaster, I am enjoying the ride a lot more (and I'm pretty sure my friends and family are, too).

You've likely noticed something similar with your routine. Although it's helpful to be aware, knowing that energy dips are part of life doesn't means it's easy to roll with the punches when we're on a drop. It's easy to feel a pull back into addiction and attempt to compensate with temporary and toxic sources of stress and stimulation. However, we can become more aware of our habits when we are able to disconnect from sources of external stress and see more clearly how we automatically default to certain behaviors that may or may not serve our intentions. When we pay attention to life's pauses and embrace our opportunity to be in the moment, we tend to face a critical challenge: After years of being constantly connected, we experience boredom when we realize we have nothing else we need or are expected to do.

We are sometimes able to push through the initial discomfort of stillness. In these cases, we can make deeper connections with our environment and ourselves and experience an enlightened sense of well-being in the moment. Silence is our best teacher, because we eliminate the self-induced pressure to be more than we are and embrace the fact that we have enough and are enough, right here and now. There is insight in the mere observation of anything. By accepting where we are and telling our brain that we have what we need, we are able to decrease the chronic stress flooding our system and allow our heart and brain to function in harmony.

Simple Stress Rules

As we get ready to embark upon the journey to building greater resilience to stress, I'd like to highlight a few simple but important principals of stress management. It is essential to keep these at the top of your mind throughout your recovery process. This is not a program you complete once and then never need to think about again. Rather, this process provides you with tools and techniques you can return to whenever you notice yourself slipping off track and feeling overwhelmed, out of balance, or run down.

- *Everything that has life has a pulse that is meant to oscillate.* It's easy to see by looking at nature that everything alive has some sort of rhythm or vibration. We can observe these waves or tides from our internal patterns, such as our circadian rhythms, to the external rise and fall of day and night. We find flow when we allow ourselves to operate in this up-and-down cycle, but when we fight it or try to override it to get more done in less time, we create imbalance and rigidity. A big part of our journey is learning to "ride life's waves" and enjoy them for what they are rather than wasting time and energy trying to resist them.

- *The higher the pulse's spikes, the lower the drops must go to get adequate recovery.* Similarly, the more stress we have at any given time, the more time we must take to relax and repair our energy. When things become more intense, and therefore require enhanced energy and resilience, it is even more important to create opportunities to take care of ourselves. Unfortunately, these challenges or storms are usually when we most neglect self-care practices, because we feel too overwhelmed to take a break. If we want to learn and grow from the difficult times, we must recharge consistently.

- *Stress is neither good nor bad; it's merely a stimulus for change.* The way in which we respond to the stress in our life is determined by our ability to adapt and change as needed to restore a sense of balance and harmony. Something we might consider negative stress can have positive outcomes—if we are able to maintain a healthy perspective on how the challenges fit into our bigger picture and seek opportunities to learn and grow throughout the process. Looking back on your life, you can likely see that your biggest periods of growth followed those that were most challenging and stressful, such as losing a job only to get a better one, ending a relationship only to become more aware of what you need in a partner, or delivering a tough presentation only to create opportunities within the organization. At the same time, consider how exhausted you've felt after a vacation. Even positive stress can throw our system out of balance if we're not prepared with the right amount of resources to facilitate the energy required to manage change.

- *Change requires energy.* Whether it's good or bad, anticipated or unexpected, any change requires energy to navigate. This is why it's critical to replenish our system regularly. Even the smallest changes or challenges can seem overwhelming and break us down when we're running on an empty tank.

- *Perception determines our reaction to stress.* Two people in the same scenario can experience drastically different effects on their brain and body depending on whether they believe they have what they need to manage the change that results from stress. For example, if you perceive stress as a challenge, your brain mobilizes the energy necessary to attack the situation. Meanwhile, someone who perceives it as a threat prepares to run away or fight it off. As we've discussed, the hormones released in response to a challenge are short term, providing energy we need to get the job done. When something is seen as a threat, the released hormones are designed to last longer, because the problem may require a longer-term solution.

Overcoming Obstacles

Before we move on to our stressaholic recovery process, let's recap some of the biggest stress management challenges and the simple solutions that will help you build a better relationship with the stress in your life.

Problem 1: You depend on stress and excess stimulation to provide the energy you need to get through the day.

Solution: Create an energy management plan that gives you real, sustainable energy and enables you to break free from relying on stress hormones for fuel.

■ ■ ■

Problem 2: Chronic multitasking dumbs you down and over-stresses your brain.

Solution: Train your brain to be more focused on a single task by practicing mental exercises such as mindfulness, meditation, and visualization.

■ ■ ■

Problem 3: Overriding your natural rhythms throughout the day because you feel like taking breaks limits your ability to get more done in less time.

Solution: Create oscillation in all that you do, including eating every 3 to 4 hours, moving your body at least every 90 minutes, and setting up 50-minute work hours that allow 10 minutes for transition and rest.

Change Your Story about Self-Care

In step 4 of the stressaholic recovery process, we use a simple practice to help reprogram the way we think about stress in life. As we transition to Part 2 of this book and begin the five-step process, I want to make sure you're committed to investing the time and energy required to create a more resilient and energy-efficient operating system. This can be extremely difficult, because it requires making "taking care of you" a priority—something that, with so many other people and tasks taking up the key spots on your priority list, can feel impossible to do.

The knowledge that we are better able to take care of others when we take care of ourselves can help with this. However, it's usually not enough when we have to choose between taking a break and finishing a project someone is waiting for; leaving for lunch and getting back to a few more people via e-mail; or going to sleep at a decent hour and prepping for an important presentation that our team is depending on us to knock out of the park. In these critical moments, we need to make sure we believe that taking care of ourselves is taking care of business. No matter what our work entails, we are our most valuable business asset. And the same rules apply when it comes to family and friends. We can give our best energy only from the overflow of our cup, not from trying to share the mere droplets we have left after giving it all away to everyone and everything else in our life.

The following messages are concepts I've found particularly helpful as I created my story around taking care of myself first. They also motivate and support me in making healthy choices for my energy and stress management amid life's most challenging struggles and storms.

1. I Am Not My Thoughts

As discussed in the previous chapter, the brain can be our best friend or our worst enemy when it comes to moving in the direction of our goals. Those 60,000 to 80,000 thoughts triggered by the brain each day are not always in alignment with how we feel or what we want. Sometimes, our brain is trying to help us survive with messages like "Just start tomorrow" or "Who are you to get a massage?" when it fears we don't have enough of what we need in the moment. Being aware of this reality can help us build in a short pause to question our thoughts. It prompts us to reflect upon the nature of what we're telling ourselves and check whether what we're saying is fully true and moving us in the direction we want to be heading. We talk more about how to rewire our thought patterns in step 4. For now, be aware that we are not our thoughts, we have the power to change our thoughts, and we can reprogram the way our brain operates. We can turn it from an enemy into a friend that we feel supports us in times of struggle, rather than feeling like we're waging war on our own mind.

2. Recovery Is Not Optional

It is your responsibility to design the lifestyle that supports your unique rhythm and balance. Other people will respect the structure you create, but only if you communicate clearly and with the right attitude, intention, and attention. In this way, you empower others to do the same, creating a more energy-efficient culture in which we can all be fully engaged in each moment we share.

3. Taking Care of Myself Is Not Selfish

If the plane were to lose air pressure within the cabin, we must put on our oxygen mask before assisting anyone else. We cannot be there to support others if we don't have our own fuel supply. Yet most people struggle to care for themselves when so many other people need caring for. We need to change our stories so that they reflect how we are better able to serve our friends, families, clients, and communities when we are healthier and happier. It is essential that we be responsible for the energy we bring to each moment.

Face the Truth

As we begin our transition to Part 2 of this book, consider one last step: facing the truth of where you are as you begin this journey.

Reading some of the challenges of stress addiction, including my story, may have you feeling like you've finally found your tribe, one that relates to the struggles of managing the chaos of your busy life. You may be able to notice consequences such as feeling fatigued, frustrated, or irritable as a result of an operating system overloaded with stress and lacking adequate recovery. But you may still not be fully aware of the damage that has been done or is continuing to be done on a cellular level in your body. For this reason, I encourage all of my clients to do a thorough physical checkup at least once a year to look under the hood and see what's really going on below the surface.

It is an exciting time in the field of biological testing, with new diagnostic tools coming into the marketplace each day. However, with any boom of information there also tends to come with it a sense of being overwhelmed as you try to decipher which programs are valuable and which are merely selling snake oil. And, of course, experiencing more stress as you try to manage your current stress doesn't seem to make sense.

To lessen this information overload, I've put together a package of current assessments that you may find helpful in exploring your unique stress response over time. This Synergy Metabolic Profile is not designed to diagnose you with any disease or disorder but rather provides you with additional information so that you can further customize your recharge and recovery program. All diagnostic tools are intended to create additional awareness as to how your body is coping with your current lifestyle and circumstances, and they should be incorporated in your overall physical health and wellness strategy with the guidance of your primary physician. If you are interested in getting more information about the Synergy Metabolic Profile, you can go to my website at www.synergyprograms .com or e-mail the Synergy team at info@synergyprograms .com. We have practitioners who are available for both in-person and virtual one-on-one and group consultations to walk you through the profile.

Regardless of whether you have the specific information about your stress response, the steps toward healing your system are the same. The remainder of this book provides you with some general guidance and practical techniques so that you can recharge your energy and reprogram your life to support a healthier, more resilient relationship with stress.

Recharge Your Energy

Between stimulus and response there is a space. In that space is our power to choose our response. In our response lies our growth and our freedom.

—Viktor Frankl

4

Step 1: Rest

To take a systemic approach to getting rest and recovery, we need to focus on the key internal triggers for the stress response: an overactive mind and an overwhelmed body.

When it comes to our cognitive workload, nothing seems to create more internal chaos than information overload. Our tendencies to be on the go nonstop and constantly connected to technology require our brains to continuously spend energy that we desperately need to replenish from time to time. Using simple mind-calming activities such as deep breathing, progressive relaxation, and meditation, we can train the brain to become more comfortable in a quiet, restorative state.

As discussed earlier, taking it easy is hard work without practice. So don't be surprised if it's uncomfortable for a while as you start trying to incorporate more downtime. It's like training your muscles in the gym: The more you practice, the easier it is to recover as you boost your cognitive fitness. Consider what it's like when you first start a workout routine. It can take several minutes to catch your breath, let alone feel strong and ready to exercise again. The same thing applies when training your brain: You need to push out of your comfort zone a little bit at a time, give yourself adequate recovery time to repair, and then push yourself again to build up strength and resilience.

The biggest indicator that we're overdoing our physical workload is chronic inflammation. Inflammation is the body's natural response to anything considered a potential threat, including stress, irritants, injuries, infections, and allergies. Even good sources of stress such as exercise can trigger an inflammatory response. When experienced short term, inflammation delivers essential elements needed to repair and rebuild the body, making it stronger over time. But similar to stress hormones, chronic exposure to inflammatory agents can lead to damage caused by heat, swelling, redness, and pain. What's worse, our inflammatory response can start to turn on our healthy cells, causing more serious illnesses.

To calm the chaos and cool our internal fire, we need to eliminate foods and other consumables (caffeine, alcohol, and nicotine) that irritate our internal chemical balance. Several items in our current food supply seem to be causing a lot of challenges for people, and food sensitivities and allergies are increasing. We'll use an anti-inflammatory nutritional approach to try to decrease foods that trigger inflammation and add nutrients that soothe our system, thereby bringing our digestive operations back into calm, restorative homeostasis, or harmony.

Finally, we need to look at how our social energy affects our state of internal balance. The quickest way to stimulate the stress response in laboratory animals is to remove them from their family or community. It's also how we torture our worst criminals, placing them into solitary confinement. Feeling isolated has been shown to be more detrimental to our health than smoking 15 cigarettes a day, triggering an inflammatory response that increases our death risk as much as being obese or living a sedentary lifestyle does.[1]

Studies are increasingly correlating social isolation to spikes in death rate from all causes, including brain diseases such as dementia and Alzheimer's disease, which can be a vicious cycle considering how lonely the process of mental decline can be on both the individual and the family.[2] Being able to reach out to friends and family in times of need is critical to feeling a sense of security and allowing the brain to rest. At the same time, we need to be careful that we're not placing excess stress or strain on our system by spending energy on people who drain us. As with all things, balance and moderation are key.

Quiet the Mind: Just Breathe

Our breath quickly shifts to a short, shallow pattern when we are stressed, which limits the amount of oxygen we get and triggers an even greater stress response. One of the quickest ways to initiate the relaxation response, which balances stress hormones and boosts positive endorphins in the brain, is to become aware of our breathing. It takes only a few moments for this intentional shift to gently but immediately cause the breath to become slower, deeper, and more calming.

The cleansing breaths of mindful breathing practices bring in more of what we need and allow us to release the stress and tension we hold in the brain and body. Practicing mindfulness not only gives us a chance to relax our operating system but also teaches us how to let go of negative thought patterns. We do more work on rewiring our mindset in step 4. For now, let's focus on training our brain to be able to relax and let go through simple meditation techniques.

To practice mindful breathing, simply close your eyes and notice the sensation you feel as you naturally breathe in and out. Direct your attention to how you feel physically, as you notice your chest and belly expand and contract as you breathe. Don't get frustrated if thoughts pop into your mind. Just acknowledge them and let them pass, focusing your attention back to your body's physical sensations.

One of the biggest challenges new meditators face is getting their mind to shut up long enough to experience stillness. I know I was turned off when I first attempted meditation. Quieting my mind for 30 minutes felt impossible when I couldn't do it for 30 seconds. However, I wanted to reap the incredible benefits of meditation that I'd heard so much about. So I began a brain training regimen of spending 3 minutes three times a day focusing on my breath until I could build up to a longer practice. As with exercising, it's important to give yourself time to push out of your comfort zone and then get enough recovery to adapt and grow stronger. After practicing for 3 minutes, try moving to 5, 10, and then 15 minutes. As you see the benefits of your efforts, you will begin to fully appreciate the investment. You'll even start to crave this time of quiet recharge.

You will most likely need some sort of focusing tool to help still your mind. There are many options. You can use a simple word, a phrase, a sound, a song, or a biofeedback device, to name a few. The important thing is that you find a way to take your mind gently away from the mental gymnastics it's accustomed to doing and give it a specific target on which to focus your mental energy. Again, similar to doing exercises in the gym, decide upon a specific time and frequency for your training regimen. Start with something that's only slightly outside your comfort zone as you build up strength to deepen your practice. Don't allow yourself to get frustrated trying to pick out the perfect tool or create the perfect meditation practice; that only triggers the stress response you're trying so hard to alleviate.

Let's discuss a few of the common mental focusing aids in more detail so that you can choose one or two to add to your routine.

Mantras

Although it may sound complicated, a mantra is simply a mind instrument used to help guide mental energy into a specific direction. Many traditional meditation practices recommend using a neutral mantra, something that has no emotional meaning or connection, to help the mind focus in a nonbiased way. This also helps alleviate the temptation to run away with thoughts triggered by particular words or past experiences, such as thinking about the word *peace* and starting to worry about all the problems in the world or thinking about the word *love* and starting to miss a loved one. These aren't bad things to think about, but we want to practice keeping our mind focused solely on what's happening in the moment. One way to use neutral words is to simply count breaths in and out. You can determine a certain number you want to count to and then count up and then back again. Or you could repeat the same number for a certain amount of time. There is no perfect way to practice this technique; the most important part is doing it.

Many people prefer to practice with a positive mantra that makes them feel peaceful or inspired. This can provide additional benefit in the brain. Positive thinking triggers the release of neurochemicals such as serotonin and dopamine, which not only make us feel good in the moment but also help us build the habit. As with any tool, the important thing is that you find what works for you and use it regularly. Examples of positive mantras might be words such as *harmony*, *balance*, or *joy* or phrases such as "Just be here now," "I am enough, I have enough," or "All is well." At the end of each of the steps in this book, I introduce a mantra that applies to the concepts discussed in the chapter, as well as provide other options you might want to try as you begin to figure out what works best for you. We discuss more mantras in step 5 when I give specific examples of oscillation practices.

Sounds

Although it's great in theory to imagine chilling out to the sounds of silence, it can be very difficult to quiet a busy and distracted mind without something specific to listen to. However, we want to be strategic about the type of sounds or noise we invite into our environment when we're trying to relax our brain. Many people try to zone out to the television, not recognizing that the busy sights and sounds stimulate the brain even when they feel as though they're not paying attention. The brain is constantly scanning our environment, trying to figure out what it may need to protect us from. Although we should all be grateful for that, this constant monitoring requires energy and potentially triggers negative thoughts and associations, taking our mind someplace we'd rather not be going when we need to relax.

When I was working on this section of the book, I became frustrated by the people who kept popping up in my space, bringing their bad vibes. Even though I regularly practice the art of what I call *distraction resistance*—trying to fully focus my energy on the task at hand and eliminate mental drifting—it's easy for me to be pulled into the stress of what people around me are dealing with: nonstop texting, cell calls full of drama, or that negative energy–vampire sensation we all occasionally experience with certain people.

This is one of the reasons that watching TV before bed poses such a problem for people who are seeking relaxation. They want to give their brain something to focus on other than running through the events of today or their to-do list for tomorrow, but a TV's bright lights and sounds cause stimulation, even while people are drifting off to sleep. Studies have shown that even a subconscious brain will light up due to noise and activity around it, costing precious energy resources right when we're trying to get our most important, and much needed, rest and repair.

One of the problems with noise coming from the TV set or from the typical work environment is that it is random and chaotic; it has no particular rhyme or reason. This is quite different from constant, repetitive, or rhythmic noise or sounds. I often laugh when I tell people I listen to noise regularly, but it's true. I have an app (yes, there's an app for that!) called Sleep Stream that allows me to choose different calming sounds such as waves, rainfall, or other sounds of nature, in addition to plain old noise. Particular sounds such as white noise or pink noise (similar background sounds with a slight variety in pitch and vibration) are designed to be steady and calming. These frequencies, and others like them, give the brain something consistent to focus on while blocking out the chaotic background sounds, thus providing no reason to be on alert.

Rhythmic sounds such as waves crashing or gentle music can also bring the brain into a calm state. You can even do some mental cross-training by combining relaxing music with inspiring lyrics to give you positive words to focus on, similar to one long mantra. I have a selection of songs that I listen to for this very purpose, and I even have one set as my ringtone to help put me in a positive mindset as I answer the phone. Although this trick doesn't always work, every little bit helps, because both stress and its counterbalance relaxation are cumulative.

Biofeedback

A third technique I've found particularly helpful for myself and my clients is using a device that provides immediate feedback on biological responses to relaxation practice. Simple programs such as EmWave or Inner Balance, both created by a company called Heartmath, enable you to see how your heart rate is responding to your breathing patterns. With either a touchpad for your finger or an ear-clip sensor, the program shows your pulse while it provides guidance to the recommended pacing for your breath. The newer Inner Balance program also lets you quickly see on your mobile device whether you're operating in a state of coherence, which is the optimal rhythmic balance between heart and brain signals—and the place where studies have shown performance to be at its peak.

Many professional athletes use biofeedback programs to train their ability to stay calm in stressful situations, especially in sports such as golf, where mental focus and resilience to stress are so critical for performance. Studies show that when stress hormones rise, they interfere with the smooth muscle functioning critical for keeping a steady, rhythmic golf swing. I recommend a few other biofeedback options in step 5 as we discuss ways to create more oscillation in your daily routine, because I believe this is one of the best ways to assess your energy and stress management throughout the day.

Now you just have to choose a technique and implement the practice. It's tempting to shorten your break time or skip it when you're facing a tough deadline, but remember: The greater the stress you're under, the more desperately you need recovery. If you're new to mindfulness meditation practices, I suggest starting with a recharge program in the same way I did: 3 to 5 minutes, three times a day for a week. To keep it simple, you may want to set aside a few minutes before breakfast, lunch, and dinner because you likely already have some sort of routine set around these time frames. Meals are also perfect times to practice relaxation, because you want your brain chemistry to be balanced enough to make healthy choices, recognize feelings of satiety, and facilitate proper digestion.

There are also some helpful apps (yes, another app for that) that send reminders throughout the day to take recharge breaks. Bloom by Mindbloom not only delivers digital reminders but also gives you the chance to customize your recharge activities by setting a video or photo to music that plays in a loop for a particular time frame. GPS for the Soul is another app that includes bio-feedback capability, using the sensor for your phone to show your heart rate, and even makes recommendations based on your results.

The way you time your recharge breaks is up to you, but I suggest that you try to schedule 10 minutes of downtime for every 50 minutes of work. I know that may sound like a lot of time to give up, but remember that this is strategic recharge time, as important as anything else you do in your day. By dividing your daily routine into these focused chunks of time, you give your brain specific boundaries: time it needs to be on and engaged and time for it to get the recovery it needs to return to the next cycle. If you're ready to build this into your routine now, it can become the core of your oscillation practice moving forward. I explain more in step 5 about how to build in these breaks, setting boundaries and expectations for others so that they respect your time and energy—and you are able to give them your best in return.

Simple Meditation Practices

Meditation experts of the past believed practice must include at least 20 minutes of focused stillness. However, new studies have shown that shorter practices of 3 to 5 minutes at a time may be as effective in reducing systemwide measures of stress, such as cortisol production and inflammation. Not only are shorter bursts of training more realistic for busy people to fit into their sched-ules, but they more accurately replicate the type of energy oscillation practice we want to build into our day. Rather than meditating for 20 to 40 minutes at one time, we can benefit more frequently from shorter relaxation breaks spread over the course of the day.

We can compare this again to working out at the gym. Exercise physiologists used to believe that we had to train for at least 30 consecutive minutes to see measurable fitness or weight management results. The new school of thought is that shorter periods might be even more effective if we're able to bring the right intensity, because we get a metabolic burst with each activity, spreading the benefits throughout the day. Also, with our busy schedules, it's more realistic to assume that we can fit in a few 5- to 10-minute sessions over the course of the day than it is to think that we can block out one longer time frame.

One of the biggest challenges people face when trying to create a meditation practice is getting hung up on how to do it right. Meditation is often associated with spiritual gurus and master teachers, so it can seem downright intimidating—even stress inducing—to try to learn. But the basic principles are quite simple, and as you experiment with different techniques, you'll quickly learn what you like and follow your internal teacher rather than trying to do things perfectly. That perfection we all seek is the type of mindset we want to eliminate through consistent meditation practice.

Let's keep this simple. Typically, meditation practice follows a few basic guidelines:

- A time frame set aside for the recharge experience (scheduled as a priority)
- A comfortable position (whatever feels relaxing to you)
- A somewhat quiet environment (free from distractions)
- A mental focusing device or technique (sound or word that is repeated)
- A nonjudgmental attitude (not critical of yourself or your process)

If you remember anything about meditation or mindfulness practice, remember that it is nonjudgmental awareness of the present moment. Learn to be aware of the here-and-now thoughts, feelings, and sensations; just notice them without judging whether they are right or wrong. The more you practice being aware of the present, the stronger your mental muscles will become and the more you'll be able to bring your full energy and engagement to the times they matter most.

Mental focusing exercises such as meditation don't just help you increase awareness. They can also harness your attention in directions that serve you. This is best done in a two-step process, first creating mindfulness awareness and then tuning in to something called your mindsight.

Neuroscientist Dan Seigel first used the term *mindsight* to describe the ability to use mental energy to direct the mind's activities.[3] Simply put, mindsight practice requires using your mind to consciously direct its attention. This unique ability to be the conductor of your own energy requires focused practice. However, it's one of the most important skills you can incorporate into your health, happiness, and performance routine.

In simple meditation, we begin with closing the eyes, relaxing the body, and tuning in to our breath to initiate the relaxation response. We then work to quiet the mind and become aware of our present-moment sensations. With practice, we learn to create mental stillness, letting the random thoughts that may pop up simply pass through like waves, without judgment or attempts to hold on. We keep our focus here during mindfulness meditation—simply being in the moment and trying to calm the body and quiet the mind. This exercise can be both healing and energizing, because it helps us restore balance in our brain chemistry while recovering priceless energy.

To create a mindsight meditation, we take the exercise one step further. Here, we focus our attention in a particular direction that brings us a desired outcome, such as positivity, gratitude, joy, patience, or relaxation, regarding a particular issue. For example:

- Target your focus on things that are positive (such as recognizing and experiencing gratitude for things you appreciate)
- Acknowledge the pull of the technological leashes in life (cell phone, computer, etc.) and strategically focus attention without checking in for certain periods
- Take time during a bumpy flight to focus mindsight on a relaxing visualization (such as driving on a bumpy road to a beach resort)
- Train the brain to see relaxation as an investment and become comfortable with not being busy

Mindsight meditation not only restores healthy balance and connection between the brain and the body; it consciously points your attention in directions that activate neural connections in your brain that rewire desired ways of thinking or being. With practice, these new pathways will lead you more quickly into the state of mind that helps you reach your goals.

If you have a few moments, go ahead and try this simple exercise now. Close your eyes and notice your breath. Become aware of the physical sensations of this breathing, and try to keep your mind from wandering; when it does, just notice it and gently bring it back to the moment. Next, think of something you feel grateful for or something you're looking forward to. Try to experience the internal shift in sensations from being in task mode to connecting to something that makes you feel good.

Imagine that positivity soaking in to your entire being and creating a more optimistic energy source for you to take with you as you return to your workday. Continue focusing on your breath as you relax into feelings of gratitude and positive anticipation for a few minutes.

Of course, the key to building any consistent ritual is practice and repetition. You must plan time to take breaks and hold your commitment as firmly as you would an appointment. Remember, you need your best energy to be the best for anyone else. Taking care of yourself is not selfish; quite the opposite is true. It's one of the only ways you can guarantee generosity toward others.

Calm the Body: Eliminate Irritants

Stress addiction is often rooted in a biochemical dependence on stimulation for energy; there simply isn't enough real energy from glucose and oxygen to keep the body and brain operating effectively. This leads to that feeling of being tired and wired at the same time: physically exhausted but mentally wound up and restless. Building time and space for rest into our schedule may seem simple in theory. However, it is the hardest step in the stress management process because it means letting go of the stress that has kept us energized for so long.

Stress doesn't just provide us with a temporary source of fuel to get things done. It also serves as a fabulous distraction tool for our brain when we'd rather not think about other things or endure painful feelings. As we slow down and start to get rest, other challenges and uncomfortable thought patterns may begin to surface. Believe it or not, that's what we want to happen. We need to work through these negative associations to release them. We can't just try to suffocate them with more stress.

Most people don't realize that their greatest stress response is triggered from stimulants within their body. There are two critical components of energy: glucose and oxygen. If we have too much or two little of either one, we push our system out of balance and into what we've come to call survival mode. It's obvious that running out of food or not being able to breathe is a death sentence, but our brain begins to fear a shortage quicker than we realize. We look at both of these critical elements as we discuss techniques of getting physical rest, stabilizing glucose with strategic nutrition, and optimizing circulation of oxygen through consistent movement and adequate sleep.

1. Balance Blood Sugar

One of the most important ways to maintain our brain's health and performance is to keep blood sugar levels stable throughout the day. The problem is that our current lifestyle seems to support the opposite of the consistency that our brain craves. We're usually rushing through our days, often unaware of hunger due to constant stress and busyness. Eating once or twice a day not only wreaks havoc on energy levels but is also certain to expand waistlines. As if that's not enough, the sugar spikes we experience throughout the day have been shown to be toxic to the brain.

Nutrition is critical to providing your system with the right quantity and quality of energy. Although your best diet strategies depend on your unique goals and priorities, the fundamentals are always the same: Eat light, eat often, and eat balanced. These simple rules keep blood sugar levels stable throughout the day and must be at the core of your program; otherwise, your energy is compromised.

We each have an ideal range of energy that we need at any given time. Although it's not important or realistic to know exactly what that amount is, we can assume based on fundamental nutritional science that we need to replenish glucose every 3 to 4 hours. When we go too long without eating, we signal to the body that there is an emergency situation and we have run out of fuel. Our body interprets this as famine or starvation and provides energy from stored glucose in the cells (protein and fat). We cannot be fully engaged when we are functioning in survival mode, because the body won't provide adequate energy to all cells—just the most essential ones. This is when you may notice yourself feeling irritable, moody, and impatient or find it difficult to concentrate on the task at hand. In an effort to conserve available resources, the brain signals a metabolic slowdown that fuels only the most critical functions, such as heartbeat and breathing. Being patient, loving, and kind just isn't that important if you're stranded on a deserted island.

Any time our glucose is elevated too much or too quickly, the body receives a signal that there's an emergency surplus, some of which it must store to keep blood sugar from staying high (which ultimately leads to serious problems such as high blood pressure, circulatory issues, and organ damage). In this case, the brain perceives a threat to survival but also embraces the idea that we have more than we need and can amp up our energy reserves (or fat cells). There is nothing better to a hungry brain than storing excess calories for the future, which is one of the reasons that cortisol, triggered by chronic stress, is so clearly linked to fat storage.

Like so many other topics we've covered in this book, balance is the key. When it comes to nutrition, too much and not enough both pull us out of balance and can cause additional stress. Few things are as toxic to the brain or as inflammatory to the body as a sudden spike in insulin caused by an energy surge (too much sugar) or the chronic cortisol stimulated by long lapses in mealtimes.

You can use meals and snacks throughout the day to provide stable glucose. Meals should give you energy for about 3 to 4 hours and consist of about four or five handfuls of food, combining protein, carbohydrate, and fruits or vegetables at each meal. This nutrient combination gives you the fast energy you need from carbohydrates while slower-processing foods that contain protein, fat, or fiber keep blood sugar from spiking too quickly. If you need some ideas for healthy, stress-free meals, visit the resources section of my website at www.synergyprograms.com. I recommend a plate that looks something like Figure 4.1.

Most people have three or four meals a day, depending on their schedule. If that's not convenient for you, snacking regularly might provide a better way to manage your blood sugar during the day. Ideally, snacks should bridge the gap between meals, keep your body going for about 2 hours, and consist of approximately 150 calories of a low-glycemic food or combination of foods. Depending on their schedules, most people have two to four snacks a day. Examples of low glycemic snacks include:

FIGURE 4.1 A Healthy Balanced Meal

- Almond butter and rice cakes or whole-grain crackers
- Hummus and pita bread
- Apple, orange, pear, or bowl of berries
- Greek yogurt, low-fat cheese, or cottage cheese and fruit
- Almonds, pistachios, cashews, walnuts, or pecans
- Small glass of almond or rice milk
- Half of an all-natural nutrition bar
- Small latte
- Steamed edamame
- Trail mix

2. Eliminate Stimulating Foods

When we start to slow down, we may experience an initial crash, which can cause us to consciously or subconsciously reach for substances that help rev us up again. Many of these come in the form of foods or food "stuffs" (overly processed consumables that look like, smell like, and taste like food but have no nutritional value). The best way to determine a good food choice is to ask whether your grandparents' grandparents would recognize it as food. Ideally it shouldn't come in a package or need a label to tell you why it's good for you. Because processed foods give us sugar and often come packaged with other highly additive substances like salt and fat, we get an immediate rush and feel energized from eating them, if only for a few moments. By temporarily eliminating these stimulating and toxic foods, we bring the body back into balance and are forced to depend on natural foods that give us more bang for our buck.

You can create a nutritional rest period by beginning with a simple elimination diet, a process that has been used for years to determine potential food sensitivities and allergies. Although there are many potential culprits in the current food supply, seven particular foods seem to cause the majority of problems across the population. I call them the stressful seven. These highly inflammatory foods are wheat, corn, soy, dairy, peanuts, sugar (including alcohol), and artificial sweeteners. Because of its stimulating effect, it's also a great idea to eliminate or at least reduce the use of caffeine for this first step of the process. Don't worry—you'll get to reintroduce all of these items into your routine further into the program. For now, you need to give your system a chance to rest.

Although it may seem like there are no options available after getting rid of everything on that list, plenty of foods make easy substitutions. Brown rice, sweet potatoes, and squash are great choices for carbohydrates, whereas eggs, almonds and other nuts and seeds (other than peanuts), legumes, and quinoa, in addition to lean meats, supply adequate protein to balance blood sugar. Optimizing intake of fresh or frozen fruits and vegetables is an important part of a balanced diet, and we focus more on these particular foods as we move into the repair phase of the program. For now, do your best to minimize processed and stimulating foods. This gives your body a better chance to get the rest it deserves.

If the elimination diet feels too shocking to your system, begin your rest process by getting rid of the most stimulating of the bunch, avoiding processed sugar, alcohol, and caffeine. Purging these irritating nutrients gives your system a better chance at obtaining rest. As you start to feel better, you might be motivated to clean up your diet even more. If you're like me, you might not want to get rid of more than what you absolutely have to based on your unique responses. If this is the case, you might consider further exploration to find out what specifically triggers an internal stress response for you.

Although several common criminals cause inflammation, you can narrow your focus further by getting a food sensitivities test. People ask me all the time whether I believe that people have developed more food allergies nowadays because we're all overly cautious and trying to blame the wrong things for our fatigue. There are so many reasons food has become more challenging; a substantial one is that many foods have been genetically modified, overly processed, or stripped of their original nutritional value. Some experts estimate that our current corn and soy production is nearly 80 to 90 percent genetically modified,[4] which means that our bodies may not recognize what we're eating is food. In addition, our soil is becoming weaker over time, so we might not be consuming the vitamins and minerals we're used to getting through our food—and instead we are being exposed to too much of what we don't want.

The causes and consequences of our current food production habits far outreach the scope of this book, but some great resources are available to you if you'd like more information. For now, it's sufficient to be aware that when food undergoes modification—including how it's treated before, during, and after preparation—it can alter the way our body responds to it. Because foods change more quickly than our digestive system can evolve, this can cause us to be out of balance. If you're interested in learning more about food allergies and intolerances, or if you'd like to do a food sensitivities test, reach out to info@synergy programs.com for additional guidance.

This can be a scary and frustrating road to explore, but don't feel overwhelmed. Take a deep breath, and start to make the simple changes we discussed earlier to balance blood sugar and eliminate key nutritional stressors for now. As you feel more rested and energized, you can continue to learn more about how you can have a positive impact on this growing problem.

3. Hydrate

People are often surprised that I don't talk more about water consumption. The truth is that most people have been lectured enough about how important it is to drink water. I've also paid close attention to the research, which suggests that we don't need to drink as much water as we once thought, because we drink other beverages that contribute to our total water intake and many foods provide water to our system. That said, I think most people feel better overall if they consume water consistently throughout the day.

The best way to determine whether you are properly hydrated is to look at the color of your urine. You are most likely adequately hydrated if it's a light shade. A darker shade of yellow is a clear sign of dehydration (unless you've recently consumed a multivitamin, which can cause a temporarily increase in urine color content). A slight amount of dehydration can impair your body's ability to function appropriately, leading to headaches, fatigue, and a sluggish digestive system, so it's worth aiming for eight glasses of water a day. Even better, keep a glass or bottle of water with you and sip from it regularly.

Here are a few other benefits to drinking water:

- Many people mistake physical signals of thirst for signals of hunger and end up eating when they're not really hungry. If you think you might be hungry, have some water first, take a few relaxing breaths, and then mindfully go into your meal or snack instead of rushing right to food.

- Drinking more water makes you use the bathroom more, which means you have to get up and walk and take breaks more regularly. This increases circulation, gives your body and brain a time-out, and increases your metabolism throughout the day.
- The bathroom is one of the only places people seem to take a break from the busyness around them (unless you're one of those people who takes their cell phone into the bathroom and continues their conversation, which I'd strongly suggest you stop doing). This makes it a perfect opportunity for you to practice a little mindful meditation.

4. Move Regularly

It may surprise you to hear that exercise can be unhealthy—and may even make you more stressed. That's because as far as the brain is concerned, you're not exercising because you want to; you're doing it because you have to. Think about it: Why would you want to expend energy exerting yourself unless it was crucial for your survival? When we're running on empty, the last thing we want to do is try to spend more of what we don't have.

But humans were built to move. It is estimated that our Paleolithic ancestors had to walk 5 to 10 miles on an average day to find food and shelter. Our bodies are therefore genetically predisposed to frequent, consistent, whole-body movement. Unfortunately, we have reduced this movement to dangerously low levels in modern times due to technological advances that make it easy to access everything we need right from our seat. Regular physical activity is a crucial part of our daily routine, because it has been shown to:

- Increase breathing and heart rate, which enhance blood flow, energy production, and waste removal.
- Stimulate the release of brain-derived neurotrophic factor, which supports the growth of new neurons.

- Increase the amount and capacity of blood vessels in the brain and body.
- Boost serotonin, a neurotransmitter that fights depression.
- Normalize sleep patterns.
- Improve self-efficacy and sense of accomplishment.
- Enhance resilience to stress over time.

Our ancient survival instincts that were so valuable thousands of years ago continue to steer us to conserve energy—specifically by eating more and moving less. The solution is therefore not to jump into an intense workout regimen. You can minimize the stress response of your body and brain by easing into more consistent daily activity that you add to your current routine. This keeps you from perceiving movement as such a huge upfront investment, meaning that your mind won't try so hard to talk you out of it.

One way to make it easier to incorporate physical activity into an already busy schedule is to gradually increase the general movement we get throughout the day. This may be more important than purposeful exercise in the gym, because the longer people sit, the higher their risk of many health problems, regardless of the amount of exercise they do. A study published in the *American Journal of Epidemiology* followed 123,000 adults over 14 years and found that those who sat more than 6 hours a day were at least 18 percent more likely to die than those who sat less than 3 hours a day.[5]

Simply standing instead of sitting can double metabolism, and walking can multiply resting metabolism fivefold. Consider the following strategies to maximize your general movement throughout the day:

- Use a headset and walk around while talking for calls longer than a few minutes.
- Use a standing desk or countertop for work.

- Modify behaviors that are usually done seated by making rules to stand at certain times, such as when watching TV or reading.
- Allow sedentary behavior only after accumulating time with activity. For example, play computer or video games after walking for 30 minutes or climbing stairs for 10 minutes.
- Start slowly by adding 5 to 10 minutes every day for a week, with a goal of an extra 1 to 2 hours of accumulated general activity each day.
- Use self-monitoring devices such as pedometers or calorie measuring applications (such as Fitbit, NikeFuel, or Body-Bug) to track progress and boost accountability.

5. Sleep Enough, Nap as Needed

Although physical activity is critical to keeping oxygen and glucose circulating throughout the day, at times we need to simply rest. We have a serious sleep problem in this country, as well as across the globe. According to recent studies, approximately 70 million Americans are affected by chronic sleep loss or sleep disorders. The annual cost of chronic sleep loss is estimated at $16 billion in health care expenses and $50 billion in lost productivity.[6]

A lack of sleep puts your body under additional stress, which may trigger increases in adrenaline, cortisol, and other stress hormones during the day. Your body is not able to undergo the proper recovery cycles when you fail to get adequate sleep. This means that you miss the opportunity for your blood pressure to dip during the evening. This may negatively affect your heart and vascular system by increasing C-reactive protein, which is released when there is inflammation in the body and has been shown to increase the risk of developing heart disease. Too little sleep also compromises immune functioning, because you fail to produce the necessary hormones and other molecules you need to fight off infection.

Sleep is not just about giving your system a rest. It is also when your body and brain do some of their most important work to repair and rebuild muscle tissue and strengthen neural connections that improve learning and memory. The area of the brain that may be most affected by sleep, or lack of it, is the prefrontal cortex, the part that's responsible for executive functioning processes such as learning, judgment, reasoning, memory consolidation, and understanding.

Sleep deprivation and sleepiness have adverse effects on performance, response times, accuracy, attention, and concentration. Lack of quality sleep has been associated with a range of quality-of-life measures, such as social functioning, mental and physical health, and even early death. It's also been correlated with obesity, increases in smoking and alcohol use, inactivity, inflammation and heart disease, and blood sugar imbalances.[7]

Most people are well aware that they should be getting more sleep but fail to make it a priority because there are so many other things they could or should be getting done. Like the scenario I described in the Introduction, we convince ourselves we'll just do one more thing before bed. Then, before we know it, hours slip by mindlessly, and sleeplessly. To get the adequate sleep we need to fully rest, it's important that we make bedtime a priority, try to stick with a consistent routine, and establish bedtime rituals that support a better quality of sleep once we get there.

Although some activities can assist you in falling and staying asleep long enough to feel rested, there are others that you should avoid before bedtime. Here are a few tips for sleeping well:

- *Go to bed early.* Some studies suggest that early to bed and early to rise is more suited to our natural rhythms.
- *Don't toss and turn.* If you have trouble falling asleep, don't just lie there. Do something relaxing until you feel sleepy.
- *Limit naps.* Napping can be helpful to recharge your energy, but be sure to keep naps brief. Nap for less than an hour and always before 3 PM.

- *Wake up at the same time on the weekend that you do on weekdays.* Though it's tempting to sleep until noon on your days off, it is best to keep timing consistent. This enables you to build a steady pattern around your sleep schedule.
- *Avoid late-day caffeine.* Don't consume caffeine in the afternoon or at night. It stays in your system for hours and can make it hard for you to fall asleep.
- *Adjust the lights in your bedroom.* Dim the lights in the evening so that your body knows it is soon time to sleep. Let in the sunlight in the morning to boost your alertness.
- *Wind down.* Take some time to wind down before going to bed. Get away from the computer, turn off the TV and your cell phone, and relax quietly for 15 to 30 minutes. Parents should keep TVs and computers out of their children's bedrooms.
- *Eat a little.* Never eat a large meal right before bedtime. It may cause you to feel drowsy, but your body will have to work hard to process all of that food, which can stimulate your system. You can enjoy a healthy snack or light dessert (such as a handful of almonds or a small bowl of frozen blueberries with yogurt) so that you don't go to bed hungry.
- *Avoid alcohol right before bed.* Although it seems like a drink or two may help you fall asleep, it may also keep you from getting the quality of sleep you need. The body quickly metabolizes alcohol, which has a stimulating effect on the brain. This disrupts sleep, even when you don't wake up.

Many people are surprised that I'm a huge fan of napping, and fortunately I have the research to back up my beliefs and justify my love of a good midday snooze. Several studies have demonstrated that taking a nap before testing cognitive skills or memory increases performance.[8] Organizations are increasingly adding napping pods and relaxation rooms for employees to use to recharge their energy. It may not be realistic for everyone to nap on the job, but you can create many of the same benefits by practicing a longer session (approximately 20 minutes) of mindfulness meditation. If you feel tired, however, give yourself permission to take a nap of 15 to 20 minutes. You may find yourself with higher levels of productivity as a result, providing a great return on your time investment.

For more information on sleep, check out the recommended reading list at the back of the book or visit www.sleepfederation .org.

Social Rest

In addition to the chemical makeup of our internal environment, what happens externally with our environment and social support triggers a shift in our body chemistry in either a positive or a negative direction. Our sense of connection with the world around us has proved to be a key energizer, even adding seven healthy years to our life span. When we feel disconnected, our brain perceives this as a threat to our survival and triggers the chronic stress response as a result. At the same time, being overly connected or feeling excess pressure to always be available can wear us down and burn us out. Like the other energy dimensions we've discussed so far, finding balance is what's best.

1. Reach Out for Social Support

When it comes to our survival instincts, being part of the right crowd may be one of the most important factors keeping us alive. Researchers often trigger the physiological stress response in animals by removing them from their social structure, because the simple act of isolating them activates stress hormones. The same applies to us—loneliness is a threat to human survival.

Considering all of the technological advances we have to keep us connected, you might think we are more social than ever.

However, this constant preoccupation with staying connected has torn apart the concept of relationships as we once knew them. We may have more breadth in our number of connections, but it's taken a toll on the depth of our relationships.

Social connection is based on how you feel, not the number of friends you have or whether you're married or single. A Harvard University study examined data from more than 309,000 people and found that a lack of strong relationships increased the risk of premature death from all causes by 50 percent—an effect comparable to smoking up to 15 cigarettes a day, and one that had a more significant negative impact than obesity and physical inactivity.[9]

When we make a positive social connection, our brain releases a feel-good chemical called oxytocin, which instantly reduces anxiety and improves focus and concentration. In 2008, Oscar Ybarra and his colleagues evaluated the social engagement of 3,600 people aged 24 to 96. They found that the more connected people were, the better they performed on a mental exam.[10] Social support has also been shown to increase cardio-vascular and immune system functioning, whereas lack of social support increased blood pressure by 30 points.[11]

Feeling lonely changes behavior as well. Studies have connected loneliness with a decrease in exercise, an increase in caloric consumption (especially comfort foods high in processed carbohydrates), and an increase in alcohol and drug consumption (both prescription and illegal). Loneliness also negatively affects immune functioning, impairs sleep, and has recently been correlated to the risk of developing Alzheimer's disease. Unfortunately, loneliness can be a vicious cycle, because it can trigger a sense of sadness that causes more isolation and an even greater sense of loneliness.

The quality of our relationships matters more than the quantity. Someone with two or three close friends may feel more fully engaged socially than someone with 20 acquaintances (or 300 Facebook connections). Although marriage was once thought to help people feel connected, it's the quality of the relationship (no surprise here), not merely marital status, that determines the potential benefit.

People with whom you have important relationships want nothing more from you than your attention. Practicing focusing exercises helps you train yourself to be more present for the people and things that matter most to you. This enables you to bring your best energy to the current moment, even when you don't have a lot of time to give. It also allows you to fully appreciate and embrace the sense of connection you're having with each interaction.

To increase your sense of connection, look at your current schedule. Try to identify times that you could either reach out to someone for a conversation or ask that person to join you on a task or activity. This is a great opportunity for cross-training, such as grabbing a friend or colleague to go for a walk so that you can exercise while you connect. You could also ask a family member to join you for a movie so that you can improve your connection while getting some relaxation—if you chose the right movie and the right family member, of course.

2. Beware of Energy Vampires

Although it's important to feel connected, too much interaction can be a drain. We all have people we care about in our lives who seem to have a dark cloud following them around. Even on the best of days, some people find a way to complain about every little thing. We want to be supportive, but it can be incredibly draining when we're already feeling run down and we don't have energy to spare. During these strategic periods of rest, it's important that we become a little selfish and protect the energy we're trying so hard to recover.

Keep in mind that this focused rest phase is not meant to last forever, so there is no need to say goodbye to those high-maintenance friends and family members you want to have around in moderation. By setting aside some time to rest and re-charge, you will be better able to give them an extra energy boost without compromising your health and happiness. For now, look at your social circle and identify people who add stress or drain your energy. You might want to let them know that you're going on a recharge break and will be unavailable for a few days just to set clear boundaries. By letting them know you're taking time for yourself and by communicating expectations, you set up healthy guidelines for yourself and for them. It may be tough initially to hold true to the limits you're setting, but as with anything else, give it a solid effort and it will become easier.

The Stress-Less Checklist

1. Take breaks every hour.
2. Turn off technology when not in use.
3. Practice mindful breathing.
4. Eat every 3 to 4 hours.
5. Decrease intake of stimulating foods.
6. Drink adequate water (aiming for eight glasses each day).
7. Get up and move at least every 90 minutes.
8. Sleep at least 7 to 8 hours each night.
9. Reach out for support.
10. Beware of energy vampires.

Putting It into Practice: Stepping Stones

At the end of each chapter in Part 2, we discuss one stepping-stone strategy that you can immediately incorporate into your practice. This technique provides you with enough structure to being training your brain and body to use the concepts discussed in the previous section while allowing you the flexibility to customize your experience as you become increasingly familiar with the application.

Stepping Stone 1: Enough

Early in my attempts to manage anxiety, I realized a significant source of stress was grounded in the idea that I wasn't enough. Perhaps what scared me even more was the notion that I was not enough in some ways and too much in others. I believe that deep down our brain triggers these insecurities with good intent: to motivate us to get more of what we need to survive (money, time, knowledge, power, influence, and other resources). Yet as we reach milestone after milestone, we naturally tend to adapt by setting the bar even higher, never quite reaching the point we think will bring us a sense of accomplishment, peace, and security.

I created a simple mantra, "I have enough, I am enough," to gently nudge my brain in a more self-compassionate direction, bringing about a renewed perspective of abundance. When we recognize that we have everything we need in this moment, we allow the brain to disarm its protective guard and experience rest, if only temporarily.

Like training a new muscle or skill, with time and repetition we can strengthen our ability to focus attention on all of the things we have, including something as simple as the air we breathe in and out in this moment, instead of obsessing about all of the things our constantly striving brain wants to have for future assurances.

Try it now. Read the following instructions, and then try to walk through the steps on your own. You can also download a guided meditation track directing this practice at www.synergy programs.com/stressaholic.

1. Get in a comfortable position and gently close your eyes.
2. Bring your awareness to the physical sensations of your breath as you inhale slowly and exhale calmly. With continued awareness on your physical body, bring the following mantra to mind: "I have enough, I am enough."

3. With each inhale, tell yourself you have enough, recognizing the security you can feel by knowing you are providing your brain and body with precious oxygen for energy. As you exhale, silently tell yourself that you are enough, remembering that right here and now you are where you're supposed to be in your life journey. There is nothing else that needs to be done in this moment. Let your to-do list drift away temporarily, knowing it will still be there after your break but that you'll have more energy to give to the tasks at hand.

4. Appreciate and embrace this moment for what it is: enough.

5. Continue your mantra, "I have enough, I am enough," for a few moments. When you feel ready, gently open your eyes and return to your day, taking with you restored confidence in the renewed energy you now bring to the world around you.

5

Step 2: Repair

The second step toward building an optimized operating system is to restore energy to repair what has been worn down over time. You can accomplish this by creating opportunities in your busy routine to do activities that replenish your energy reserves. These strategic recovery techniques are more than just a time-out; they should leave you feeling like you have more energy than before you started. It is important to continue your rest practices so that you're still encouraging oscillation, cellular restoration, and periods of disengagement. By incorporating these simple repair practices into your routine, you increase the benefit you get from essential nutrients that holistically nourish your system.

Recovery can be different for different people based on what fills their energy cup, so to speak. I once talked my mom into getting a massage, and she thought it was awful. However, she enjoys gardening, whereas I intentionally live in a condo with no weeds to pull. The important thing about recovery is that you find something that you can rely on to restore energy when you're feeling depleted. You may want to build up a recovery toolbox with different options based on how you're feeling in the moment, because it may change from one cycle to the next or over time.

Sometimes you might want to do something passive, like getting a massage or other spa treatment, listening to a book on tape, or taking a nap. On other occasions, you may find it most helpful to do something a more active, like going for a nature walk, doing tai chi or another gentle form of movement, or even cleaning the house. It may sound absurd to undertake that kind of chore for recovery. However, the physical movement and mindless productivity not only improve circulation but also can help clear stress-inducing clutter, giving you a sense of accomplishment that boosts feel-good chemicals in the brain.

This would be a great time to jot down a few things that you enjoy doing that can help you restore energy when you're feeling run down. Consider both passive and active strategies, and make a list of your top three to five techniques. If you get stuck, talk to friends about what they do to recharge throughout the day, and set up a time to join them and try something new. You may be surprised by the activities you enjoy, and you always get an additional boost of nourishing oxytocin in the brain by having someone else along for the experience.

Nourish the Mind: Practice Gratitude

We're constantly being bombarded by negative stories in the press, which makes it easy to remain in a stressed state of mind. When we experience overwhelming stress, our brain becomes rigid and we lose flexibility and creativity. We also have a tendency to stay focused on the negatives around us and miss out on the joy of what's good in life. Our brain is naturally wired this way to help us survive, so don't beat yourself up about being pessimistic. Negative influences have a stronger impact on us than positive ones, because they trigger the natural stress response that's designed to protect us from threats in our environment. This is important when we need to be able to respond quickly and intuitively, such as to a fire blazing through our home or a truck veering toward us on the road. But we can get caught in this survival mindset in our daily, stress-filled lives. As a result, it breaks us down physically, emotionally, mentally, and spiritually.

That's one reason practicing gratitude is so important and is one of my top strategies for keeping our system healthy and functioning at its best: The more often we remind ourselves about what's good in life, the more optimistically we're able to look at the world. If you see more positive, more positive will come to you (or you'll just be more aware of it). Focus on the negative, and that's what you'll get.

Studies show that people who are more grateful have higher levels of well-being. They are happier, less stressed, and generally more satisfied with many areas of their lives, including their relationships. Gratitude might be one of the strongest predictors of happiness. The most exciting thing about this resource is that the latest research in positive psychology suggests that gratitude is something that we can train ourselves to automatically incorporate.[1]

In one study, Martin Seligman's group of researchers looked at a variety of happiness training methods to determine which were the most effective. Out of the strategies tested, the largest spike in positivity was seen in the group that wrote and delivered a letter of thanks to someone in their life. This improved happiness scores by 10 percent, and the impact of the intervention lasted up to a month after the visit. The longest-lasting effects were seen in the group that wrote in a journal each day three things for which they were grateful. Not only did these participants show increases in happiness, but their scores continued to increase each time they were evaluated after the initial intervention, often showing the biggest benefit around six months later. Because the results were so beneficial and required little time investment, many of the participants decided to voluntarily continue well beyond the initial one-week study.[2]

Here are a few simple but impactful ways to practice gratitude:

- Write down three things you're grateful for each morning to start your day.
- Discuss with a friend or family member three things you feel blessed by at the end of the day.
- Write a note of thanks to someone who has positively affected your life.
- Keep a blessings journal with a list of things you feel grateful for.
- Let people around you know that you appreciate them regularly.

What are you grateful for today? Do a self-study: This week, write down three things you're grateful for each morning before you start your workday. For an added happiness and oxytocin boost, each evening share three things you enjoyed about your day with a friend or family member.

Show Self-Compassion

Another way to practice gratitude is to show appreciation to ourselves through self-care rituals and healing therapies such as massage, pedicures, manicures, or other spa services or activities we might usually consider self-indulgent. If these types of pampering activities aren't your thing, you may prefer playing cards with friends, or ruining a good walk with a game of golf (my fellow golfers will know just what I mean here). Why not indulge and spend some time adding restorative energy into your tank? As I mentioned earlier in the book, massage has been a lifesaver for me. When I was going through my worst anxiety experiences, I recognized that I needed to do something to try to restore balance to my overexcited brain and body. Although it took some time to get used to allowing myself to relax, massage has become a strategic practice. Whenever I'm feeling stuck, massage is my go-to strategy to help relax my brain and quiet my mind. As I let go of expectations, I'm able to experience creativity and insight well beyond what happens when I'm in a thinking, analytical mode. But remember, there is no one-size-fits-all approach when it comes to recovery. Experiment and see what works best for you.

Nourish the Body: Eat Energy-Enhancing Foods

Although it goes against our instincts of getting as much volume for as cheap as we can, we need to retrain ourselves to recognize the importance of quality over quantity when it comes to nutrition. Finding cheap food is not challenging for most people these days. However, to make food inexpensive, it usually requires a laboratory to make it tasty, portable, and able to withstand a long shelf life. If you eat healthy, real foods most of the time, you are getting a greater return on investment with regard to quality nutrients. I suggest that you aim to have about 80 to 90 percent of your food come from natural sources, and then 10 to 20 percent can be whatever you want. This gives you the nutrients your body needs but also keeps you from feeling deprived.

Your choices for meals and snacks can make a big difference in how your body and brain perform for you. As discussed in the previous chapter, eating in a steady, stable, and balanced way is the most important factor. Once you have that down, then you can increase your energy return by eating high-impact foods that have been shown to provide benefits to your system beyond giving you the calories you need.

Of all the diets out there, I find that the Mediterranean diet provides the highest nutritional return on investment from both a brain and a body perspective. Many foods included in this diet are anti-inflammatory, help optimize blood flow, and decrease overall wear and tear. Generous amounts of vegetables provide the vitamins, minerals, antioxidants, and polyphenols that reduce oxidative damage in the body and brain, which may contribute to most major health concerns, including heart disease, diabetes, dementia, and cancer. Some studies show that people who eat a Mediterranean diet are less likely to experience depression and may have a reduced risk of developing dementia and Alzheimer's disease.[3] The amount of healthy fats and complex carbohydrates make this nutrition regimen satisfying—and might help people trying to lose weight or sustain weight loss.

The whole-grain carbohydrates, lean protein, and healthy fat of the Mediterranean diet are excellent at keeping the body functioning at its best and sustaining a balance of nutrients. Eating this way stabilizes blood glucose, which gives the body and brain a consistent and reliable source of fuel. In addition to maintaining energy levels, the quality of nutrients is also high impact. These foods provide monounsaturated fat, omega-3 fat, lean protein, fiber, and many vitamins, minerals, and other protective nutrients such as antioxidants and polyphenols. At the same time, there is a decreased focus on foods that may be harmful to our health, such as saturated fat, trans fat, and highly processed carbohydrates.

The Mediterranean diet specifically includes the following:

- *Monounsaturated fat:* olive oil, olives, canola oil, avocado, almonds, and other nuts, and seeds
- *Omega-3 fat:* fatty fish, some nuts and seeds, and some eggs
- *Lean protein:* fish, moderate amounts of eggs and poultry, and low-fat cheese and yogurt
- *Fiber:* beans, lentils, fruits, vegetables, whole-grain bread, cereal, and pasta
- *Vitamins and minerals:* fruits, vegetables, whole-grain bread, cereal, and pasta
- *Antioxidants and polyphenols:* fruits, vegetables, dark chocolate, moderate amounts of red wine and other alcohol, coffee, and tea

Some of the best anti-inflammatory foods are wild salmon; green vegetables such as kale and spinach; cruciferous veggies including broccoli, Brussels sprouts, and cauliflower; dark berries such as blueberries, raspberries, and acai; soothing oils such as extra virgin olive, coconut, and avocado oils; and spices such as turmeric, garlic, and ginger. Here's my personal top 10 foods list:

1. *Dark chocolate:* This one's always a crowd pleaser, so why not start with dessert? Similar to darkly colored berries, the cocoa bean is one of the highest sources of polyphenols, which are shown to decrease inflammation, boost immune function, and improve circulation.[4] The cocoa bean is nature's most concentrated source of theobromine, a compound closely related to caffeine. But unlike caffeine,

theobromine has only a mild stimulatory effect on the central nervous system, which may be beneficial for increasing energy and focus without the caffeine crash many people experience (especially caffeine-sensitive individuals). The recommendation has long been to choose products with at least 70 percent cacao for the highest nutrient value. Dark chocolate's nutrients may be destroyed by heat processing, which is the method of choice for most U.S. chocolate producers. Some premium chocolatiers use the more expensive cold press system to retain nutrient value, but beware of chocolate with added sugar, salt, or fat, some of the most highly addictive substances to the brain. These can cause glucose spikes and weight gain from overconsumption.

2. *Leafy greens and cruciferous veggies:* I could write an entire chapter solely on the benefits of leafy green and cruciferous vegetables. Both are incredibly high in anti-inflammatory phytonutrients such as vitamins A, C, and E; beta-carotene; lutein; zeaxanthin; and folate. Some, such as collards and kale, are particularly rich in calcium and potassium, both of which are important for blood pressure management and preventing osteoporosis. Veggies are also high in insoluble fiber, which aids in digestion and keeps things moving smoothly. Cruciferous vegetables such as broccoli and cauliflower contain specific compounds that have been shown to aid in detoxification and may help eliminate carcinogenic (cancer-promoting) substances in the body.[5] I always suggest starting a meal with a good source of fresh or frozen vegetables as the foundation of your plate and then adding healthy protein and fat to optimize the health-promoting benefits. For example, focus your meal on a generous portion of salad mixed with quinoa or other whole grains, or use stir-fry veggies with some olive oil, spices, and lean fish or grass-fed beef. Consider your produce to be the main dish and other foods as sides, instead of the other way

around, to create a richer return on investment from the calories you consume.

3. *Fruit, especially berries:* Packed with brain-boosting benefits, blueberries seem to take the cake when it comes to reliable research touting their benefits. They rate as one of the foods highest in antioxidant value. Some studies show that blueberry consumption may help to heal oxidative damage in the brain, helping to reduce memory loss and potentially slowing other types of cognitive decline.[6] All berries— including raspberries, blackberries, cranberries, and strawberries—are high in the phytonutrients that provide anti-inflammatory protection. Rich in the polyphenol compound resveratrol, which has been shown to be beneficial for enhancing the flexibility of arteries, optimizing circulation, and decreasing inflammation, grapes and cherries come in a close second to the berry family. Tropical fruits such as pineapple and papaya provide protein-digesting enzymes, in addition to antioxidant vitamins such as C and E.

4. *Fatty fish:* Studies have shown that eating fatty cold-water fish such as salmon, mackerel, sardines, and tuna, which are high in omega-3 fatty acids, may decrease triglycerides, lower blood pressure, reduce blood clotting, boost immunity, improve arthritis symptoms, and enhance learning ability in children. Eating one to two servings of fish weekly also appears to reduce the risk of heart disease, particularly sudden cardiac death.[7] If you do not like fish, you can boost your level of healthy omega-3 fat by eating other sources such as flaxseeds and walnuts; however, you need to eat a lot more to get the same health benefits. You may want to try supplementing with fish oil, approximately 1,000 to 2,000 mg a day for general health and more if you have high triglyceride levels. As with any dietary change, you must consult with a doctor before consuming supplements,

especially in high doses, because there may be counter-indications with other medications or procedures. For example, fish oil can be a natural blood thinner and should not be consumed before surgery.

5. *Nuts and seeds (ideally other than peanuts):* Nuts and seeds are rich in healthy fats, high in fiber, and easy to incorporate into your diet. You can enjoy a variety of them plain, or toss them into a mix with dried fruit like cranberries, plums, or coconut for a healthy snack. Don't forget about healthy nut butters, such as almond butter, as great replacements for peanut butter, which may be higher in toxins and pro-inflammatory omega-6 fats.

6. *Beans and lentils:* The soluble fiber found in beans and lentils can help decrease stressful situations such as high blood sugar, unhealthy cholesterol, and triglycerides. These are also low-glycemic foods, which means that they take longer to break down into usable energy, preventing the blood sugar spikes and crashes that can trigger inflammation. Beans are low in fat, calories, and sodium but high in complex carbohydrates and dietary fiber, and they offer modest amounts of essential fatty acids. They are also an excellent source of protein; simply combine them with grains such as barley or oats to provide all the amino acids necessary to make a complete protein for vegetarians, who do not use animal sources of protein for their meals. One cup of cooked beans a day provides as much as 15 grams of dietary fiber, approximately half of the recommended daily value needed for optimal health and digestion.

7. *Eggs:* Long considered a nutritional no-no, eggs have become a favorite protein source due to their high levels of choline, an essential nutrient that plays a critical role in the normal development of the brain, especially its memory center, the hippocampus. Eggs are rich in protein and B vitamins, and some studies show they may boost the

production of healthy forms of cholesterol. Opt for eggs that are derived from grass-fed, free-range hens—preferably with a diet rich in omega-3 fats—for added benefit.

8. *Olive, avocado, and coconut oils:* Olive oil is a staple of the Mediterranean diet. Rich in monounsaturated fat and polyphenols, virgin olive oil can be used as a fabulous dressing for cold dishes. Fresh avocado is an excellent spread or garnish, or you can use its oil for slightly higher-temperature cooking. Although it's high in saturated fat, which has been found to increase inflammation when consumed via animal products, coconut oil has been shown to decrease inflammatory markers.[8] Its high smoke point makes it more stable and less likely to become rancid with heat, which also makes coconut oil a good option for cooking at higher temperatures.

9. *Sweet potato:* Similar to its cousins, exotic fruits and vegetables, the sweet potato is a good source of complex carbohydrates, beta-carotene, manganese, and vitamins B_6 and C, as well as dietary fiber. Working in concert, these nutrients are powerful antioxidants that help heal inflammation in the body. (Sweet potato fries, one of my favorite indulgences, are not a health food and should be enjoyed only in moderation.)

10. *Spices:* Although they're often neglected when we're in a hurry, spices such as turmeric, garlic, ginger, cinnamon, and cloves not only add significant anti-inflammatory benefits but also enhance the flavor and experience of food.

The Experience of Eating

One part of the Mediterranean diet that's often left out of conversations is the lifestyle that supports the dietary components. A diet includes more than what we eat; it also pertains to how we eat. Food is more than the sum of its parts in this lifestyle;

the Mediterranean diet approach is about nature, culture, community, friends, and family. It involves technique, preparation, garnishes, color, texture—all the seemingly minor details that add positive energy to the foods we eat while creating a healthier, more enjoyable emotional experience.

Our busy schedules can make it difficult to prepare our own foods every day or to slow down enough to add the special touches that make food more fun. But consider these efforts to be yet another energy investment that can provide us with a significant return. After all, it's not just the nutrients we put into our body but also the way our internal system is prepared to receive, process, and digest those nutrients that make a difference. When we're full of stress hormones, we tend to store more calories as fat for the upcoming emergency our brain believes is ahead. When we're in a relaxed state of mind, however, our body is able to take the time it needs to fully digest and synthesize nutrients into the body for more optimal energy production.

Incorporate Daily Moderate Exercise

Although it may appear that more people are going to the gym these days, only about one in four gets the recommended minimum 30 minutes of moderate activity each day.[9] Statistics show that about half of those who begin a new exercise routine drop it within six months to a year.[10] As we discussed in the previous chapter, the last thing your brain wants to do if you're running on empty is spend more energy. However, you've probably felt exhausted but pushed yourself to get some physical activity— and ended up feeling energized. When it comes to exercise, you have to spend some energy to get a greater return.

One of the challenges for stress addicts is that exercise becomes one of the only ways to boost cortisol when adrenal systems are stressed. After years of burning the candle at both ends, we sometimes need to push ourselves to extremes to feel anything. Studies have shown that overtraining a tired system can cause more harm than good. For instance, lab animals that were forced to exercise did not show any of the health benefits received by the comparison group that exercised voluntarily.[11] Feeling like a rat on a treadmill is as bad as it sounds.

Recommendations for an optimal amount of exercise vary depending on your goals. For example, the American Heart Association suggests getting at least 30 minutes of moderate activity every day of the week.[12] This makes sense; the more you move, the better your circulation, the better oxygen gets transported to the cells, the better you're able to use glucose, and so on. However, the American College of Sports Medicine recommends 30 to 60 minutes of moderate activity daily or 20 minutes a day of intense exercise.[13]

I encourage you to take your physical activity progress slowly during the repairing phase, making sure you build in adequate recovery time. You can increase your general activity with techniques discussed in the preceding chapter to make sure you're moving frequently throughout the day without extra stress on your system. In the next chapter, we look at ways you can increase your fitness level through strategic interval training that pushes you beyond your comfort zone for a short period to stimulate growth.

Have More Fun

Although most people don't play games with the intent of improving their health, recent studies have demonstrated that having fun and laughing can have tremendous impact on all dimensions of health: physically, emotionally, mentally, and spiritually. "Laughing groups" have become a worldwide phenomenon; there are more than 6,000 social laughter clubs in about 60 countries.[14] Our physical body cannot differentiate between real laughter in response to something we genuinely find funny and unconditional laughter that is merely brought on by our intention to laugh. Practiced with a group, this laughter quickly becomes contagious, and the impact is substantial.

Physically, laughter encourages the relaxation response. This physiological reaction is triggered by deep breathing and stimulates the production of feel-good chemicals like serotonin and dopamine. It also decreases toxic stress hormones, such as cortisol, that are constantly building up in our system. Laughter enhances our body's immune functioning by increasing the production of natural killer cells that destroy viruses and disease along with gamma interferon (a disease-fighting protein), T cells, and B cells. Some researchers estimate that laughing 100 times is equal to 10 minutes on a rowing machine or 15 minutes on an exercise bike.[15] People often hold in negative emotions that build up during the day, which can have a toxic effect on the body, mind, and spirit. Laughter creates a type of emotional release, providing many people with a cathartic experience.

The Energy Repair Checklist

- Practice gratitude.
- Get a massage or other healing therapy.
- Eat energy-enhancing foods.
- Incorporate moderate exercise daily.
- Have more fun (social support, laughter, and play).

Stepping Stone 2: Gratitude

As we consider ways to nourish the body and mind, let's take a moment to check in and think about what we feel grateful for in this moment. It can be overwhelming to imagine all the things we could or should be doing to help repair our internal system from the stress in our lives. When we get too focused on our to-do list, we easily slip back into survival mode and begin to worry again about getting things done rather than enjoying the experience in the moment.

Thinking about things for which we're grateful not only connects us with what's good in our lives but also shifts our brain out of logical, analytical doing mode and into a more healing, soothing mode of being. At the same time, remembering what we appreciate about life triggers the release of positive endorphins in the brain that help balance our internal chemistry. Consider your gratitude training to be another simple way of adding nourishing chemicals to the brain, similar to adding fertilizer to soil, to enhance its richness and strengthen its resolve.

Try it now. Read the following instructions, and then walk through the steps on your own. You can also download a guided meditation track directing this practice at www.synergyprograms .com/stressaholic.

1. Get in a comfortable position and gently close your eyes.
2. Bring your awareness to the physical sensations of your breath as you inhale slowly and exhale calmly. With continued awareness on your physical body, direct your attention toward something you feel grateful for, saying to yourself: "In this moment, I am grateful."
3. Picture the person, place, or thing that you most appreciate having in your life at this moment. It can be someone you love, an opportunity that you feel thankful for, or an experience you have enjoyed or look forward to. Try to imagine as many details as you can about what you feel most grateful for right now, and see whether you can feel the changes in your body and mind as you let the magnitude of this gratitude settle in at the deepest level of your being.
4. With each inhale, think about the object of your appreciation in rich detail, letting the positive endorphins flood your brain and start to wash through your body with a warm

sense of nourishing energy as you say to yourself, "In this moment." As you exhale, silently tell yourself, "I am grateful," recognizing the sense of calm excitement you feel right here and now.

5. Appreciate and embrace this moment for what it is: gratitude.

6. Continue your mantra, "In this moment, I am grateful," for a few minutes. When you feel ready, gently open your eyes and return to your day, taking with you restored confidence in the renewed energy you now bring to the world around you.

6

Step 3: Rebuild

To fully recharge your energy, it's crucial to train your brain and body to work even better than they have in the past. You're not just restoring balance here; you're creating the best possible operating system by building up energy reserves and strengthening resilience. To do this, you create strategic training stress that requires you to push a little outside of your comfort zone, using both physical and cognitive exercises designed to optimize your performance. Keep in mind that as you start to build up your energy reserves, it becomes even more critical to continue to invest strategically in relax and repair techniques during the day. If you stretch out of your comfort zone to train without having the necessary energy resources, you may find yourself starting to break down again. You might even become dependent on stress hormones and overstimulation to keep you going, as you have in the past.

To optimize your training and get the most return on your investment, you need to continue to build in reliable recharge breaks throughout the day, regardless of whether you feel like you need them. I can promise that you do.

Strengthen the Mind: Cognitive Training

When we think of the word *fitness*, we usually think of physical fitness, or our body's ability to do work. The elements of physical fitness include three primary areas: strength, flexibility, and endurance. To be fit, you need to develop and maintain all three through strategic training. The brain is another part of our body that we need to keep in shape if we want it to function at its best. The fitter the brain is, the more energy efficient it becomes, and the easier it is to do important mental tasks, such as focusing attention, remembering information, and being creative.

The elements required for our brain to be fit are the same as those required for our bodies. To be mentally sharp and able to focus on what's most important to us—and to be able to sustain that focus over time—we need to train our cognitive strength to be fully present in the moment, our flexibility to be adaptable and creative, and our endurance to sustain performance and resilience as we age. Paying attention to these dimensions of our mental energy not only helps us be as sharp as we can in our current career and our relationships but also gives us the edge to be healthy and happy as we age.

I discuss the three elements of cognitive fitness in more depth in my previous book, *The SHARP Solution: A Brain-Based Approach for Optimal Performance*. If you're interested in more details about how to holistically train your brain to be healthy and fit, I encourage you to check out that resource or visit the training programs available for free at www.synergyprograms .com/braingym.

In previous chapters, we discussed a few cognitive fitness strategies that help us rest and repair our mental energy—deep breathing, relaxation exercises, and gratitude practices. To continue our work, let's focus on a few more techniques that help us to gently rebuild our cognitive reserves for added resilience.

Creating Coherence

Newer research has pointed to a significant measure of the interactions between autonomic nervous system dynamics that control our stress and those that control our relaxation responses, called heart rate variability (HRV). In addition to measuring our heart rate, HRV accounts for the activity of both the sympathetic (stress) and the parasympathetic (recovery) system, as well as the synchronization between the two. Put simply, this is like being able to test our ability to apply both our internal gas pedal for fuel and our brake pedal when we need to slow down or come to a complete stop.

HRV devices use a pulse sensor, usually placed on the fingertip or ear, to provide instant feedback on the current rhythmic patterns occurring at a cardiovascular level. Research by the Institute of HeartMath has identified a distinct mode of functioning frequently associated with the experience of sustained positive emotion that the organization calls *physiological coherence*. For this purpose, *coherence* is used to describe a mode that encompasses a range of internal shifts that emerge when the body is able to bring operations into a more harmonious state. According to HeartMath, physiological coherence helps synchronize the two branches of the autonomic nervous system (the "gas pedal" and the "brake pedal"), increases communication between the heart and the brain, and creates a harmonious relationship among the various internal rhythms of our oscillatory systems (such as heart rate, breath rate, brain waves, and blood pressure).[1]

Research shows that increasing heart rhythm coherence is linked to many factors that contribute to wellness. Coherence is more than simple relaxation; it is a focused state of dynamic balance between the sympathetic and the parasympathetic branches of the autonomic nervous system. You can learn to function in this state while at rest, work, or play. Because HRV training is easy and self-directive, it can be a powerful tool to help generate an increased state of coherence at will, thereby reducing stress and improving health, well-being, and performance. There are several HRV training devices available for use. My favorites include the EmWave and Inner Balance programs, both by HeartMath (www.heartmath.com); the free iPhone app GPS for the Soul; and My Calm Beat by My Brain Solutions (www.mybrainsolutions.com/mycalmbeat). An added feature of My Calm Beat is a simple series of tests you can use to identify your unique ideal breath rate, which allows you to set the device to train within the parameters best suited for your preferences.

Strengthen the Body: Interval Training

Although there are many ways to strengthen our physical system, one technique that has been shown time and again to boost both physical and mental performance is cardiovascular or aerobic training. According to the Human Performance Institute, cardiovascular training is the most efficient and effective method for increasing our aerobic fitness and energy-generating capacity.[2] Any activity that involves continuous movement can be considered aerobic—including running, cycling, swimming, and walking, in addition to dancing, playing sports, and circuit training with weights or body weight. Ideally, we want to perform cardiovascular training a minimum of three times a week, with no more than two days of rest between workouts. The intensity of the exercise is the key factor in determining the return on investment.

You can typically measure intensity by your perceived exertion or your heart rate. Purchasing and regularly using a heart rate monitor is one of the best investments you can make to support your fitness program, because it gives you an objective measure of your target training zone. Your estimated maximum heart rate can be calculated by taking 220 minus your age. According to the American College of Sports Medicine, the target heart rate zone for maximizing cardiovascular improvements is 70 to 90 percent.[3] If you are unable to measure your heart rate, you can use your perceived exertion, which is a score you assign to how you're feeling in the moment by rating your effort level on a scale of 1 to 10. Consider a moderate walk a 4 or 5 and a full-out sprint that you could sustain only for a few seconds to be your maximum effort.

Age (in years)	70% Target Heart Rate (in beats per minute)	90% Target Heart Rate (in beats per minute)	Age (in years)	70% Target Heart Rate (in beats per minute)	90% Target Heart Rate (in beats per minute)
20	140	180	50	119	153
21	139	179	51	118	152
22	139	178	52	118	151
23	138	177	53	117	150
24	137	176	54	116	149
25	137	176	55	116	149
26	136	175	56	115	148
27	135	174	57	114	147
28	134	173	58	113	146
29	134	172	59	113	145
30	133	171	60	112	144
31	132	170	61	111	143
32	132	169	62	111	142
33	131	168	63	110	141
34	130	167	64	109	140
35	130	167	65	109	140
36	129	166	66	108	139
37	128	165	67	107	138
38	127	164	68	106	137
39	127	163	69	106	136
40	126	162	70	105	135
41	125	161	71	104	134
42	125	160	72	104	133
43	124	159	73	103	132
44	123	158	74	102	131
45	123	158	75	102	131
46	122	157	76	101	130
47	121	156	77	100	129
48	120	155	78	99	128
49	120	154	79	99	127

Continuing the theme that we've been focused on through-out this book, interval training incorporates the notion of oscil-lation by using periods of higher intensity and lower intensity to create a cyclic format. Many studies have cited the benefits of interval training over other types of workouts. This approach gives exercisers the chance to push higher out of their comfort zone, which triggers an even greater initial stress response and then gives the opportunity to decrease intensity for periods of active rest so that the body learns to get into recovery mode more quickly over time. These spikes of intensity increase metabolism and may burn more calories and fat than more static types of exercise routines.[4]

There are numerous advantages to using interval training during your cardio workout:

- Your heart and lungs become bigger, stronger, and better able to take on intense challenges more efficiently and to recover more quickly.
- You boost your metabolism, causing you to burn extra calories for up to 48 hours after your training session (as explained further in the next section).
- A constantly changing workout is more interesting.
- It's easier to get started with an interval training workout by focusing on the short amount of time for each sprint (1 to 3 minutes).
- You can get maximum return on your investment by going for quality over quantity.

Sample Interval Training Workout

You can always adjust your training segments to keep things changing and keep the body challenged; they do not have to be the same length. You can also combine cardiovascular and strength training by stepping off the machine during the recovery phase and doing light dumbbell or resistance band exercises. Consider the following sample interval training workout.

Interval	Type of Workout	Target Heart Rate	Perceived Exertion (1–10)
00:00–3:00	Warm-up	50%	5–6
03:00–6:00	High intensity	80%–90%	8–9
06:00–9:00	Moderate	70%	7
09:00–12:00	High intensity	90%	9
12:00–15:00	Moderate	70%	7
15:00–18:00	High intensity	90%	9
18:00–21:00	Moderate	70%	7
21:00–24:00	High intensity	90%	9
24:00–27:00	Moderate	70%	7
27:00–30:00	Cool down	50%–60%	5–6

Once you get used to the concept of interval training, you can easily mix up your workout to keep the body challenged, such as in the next sample workout. Depending on what you like to do, you can vary several factors of your exercise:

- *Type:* treadmill, elliptical machine, rowing machine, body weight circuit, and so on
- *Frequency:* three times versus five or six times a week
- *Duration:* 20 minutes at higher intensity (sprint versus jog) with perceived exertion of 8 to 10 or a longer workout at a lesser intensity, like 45 minutes with perceived exertion 7 to 9; you can also modify the length of the actual sprint and recovery segments.

Interval	Type of Workout	Target Heart Rate	Perceived Exertion (1–10)
00:00–3:00	Warm-up	50%	5–6
03:00–6:00	High intensity	80%–90%	8–9
06:00–8:00	Moderate	70%	7
08:00–10:00	High intensity	90%	9
10:00–12:00	Moderate	70%	7
12:00–13:00	Sprint	90%–95%	9–10
13:00–15:00	Moderate	70%	7
15:00–16:00	Sprint	90%–95%	9–10
16:00–17:00	Moderate	70%	7
17:00–19:00	High intensity	90%	9
19:00–21:00	Moderate	70%	7
21:00–24:00	High intensity	80%–90%	
24:00–26:00	Moderate	70%	7
26:00–27:00	Sprint	90%	9
27:00–30:00	Moderate	70%	7

It has been well established that your body expends a greater amount of energy bringing itself back to a pre-exercise state after intense exercise, a concept summarized by excess postexercise oxygen consumption (EPOC). The specific functions that use more oxygen, and therefore burn more calories, include replenishing oxygen stores, resynthesizing phosphagen (adenosine triphosphate phosphocreatine), removing lactate, and increasing ventilation, blood circulation and body temperature above pre-exercise levels. EPOC's magnitude depends on the intensity and duration of exercise. It generally takes between 15 minutes and 48 hours for the body to return to its pre-exercise state. Intensity is the biggest factor in the amount of calories consumed during exercise and afterward through EPOC.

A lot of people don't have enough time to work out all at once as much as they'd like. The good news is that several studies have demonstrated that EPOC is greater after splitting a workout into two shorter bursts of exercise than after one longer workout.[5] Like much of what we've discussed in this book, it's crucial to stay focused on the quality of energy we bring to the time we're training. It's not enough to merely go through the motions to check off another box on our to-do list. Too many people spend too much time in the gym without getting the results they desire because their focus is distracted. When you're investing in rebuilding your system, both mentally and physically, you have to be completely engaged in the activity at hand. Then, you can quickly move on to more restful and relaxing recovery strategies to help you get the most benefit from your time and energy investment.

The Optimal Oscillation Checklist

- Schedule recovery breaks, and make them a priority.
- Create coherence with HRV training.
- Increase energy through physical interval training.

Stepping Stone 3: Let in, Let Go, and Find Your Ideal Flow

Life is a series of beats. Everything that has life has a natural rhythm of ups and downs, giving and receiving, stress and recovery. We can find our optimal performance pulse by tuning in to our natural oscillation process, which is facilitated by our internal rhythms—our inhales and exhales, heartbeats, blood sugar fluctuations, brain waves, and so on. Even our energy levels naturally rise and fall during the day.

Look at your personal routine. When do you notice yourself feeling most energized? When during the day do you experience energy dips or crashes? Although feeling burned out or exhausted is not natural, we have to expect our energy levels to naturally rise and fall in alignment with our resources. Often, our energy is greatest in the morning when we first arise and cortisol levels are highest. There's usually a dip in the afternoon during a circadian rhythm drop (otherwise known as the nap zone, typically felt around 3:00 or 4:00 PM). Then there's a steep decline in the evening as cortisol levels drop and sleep-inducing melatonin begins to increase.

When we fight our natural rhythms—or worse, try to override them with stimulants such as caffeine or stress hormones—we essentially force our system to slowly adapt to being on all of the time. Although we may consider this a good thing for productivity, we must recognize that the results of nonstop stimulation are toxic to both the brain and the body. They rob us of the time and energy we're trying to conserve.

Like training a new muscle or skill, time and repetition allow us to strengthen our ability to recalibrate our natural rhythm. We're able to create a more optimal pulse or flow that provides us with greater amounts of energy for short periods. In addition, we use a consistent recharge process to invest energy back into our system for resilience and sustainability.

Try it now. Read the following instructions, and then walk through the steps on your own. You can also download a guided meditation track directing this practice at www.synergyprograms .com/stressaholic.

1. Get in a comfortable position and gently close your eyes.
2. Bring your awareness to the physical sensations of your breath as you inhale slowly and exhale calmly. With continued awareness on your physical body, imagine on your next inhale that you are delivering fresh, energizing air, expanding upward within your head to fill each nook and cranny of your busy brain. As you fill your head and nourish your brain with clean, invigorating oxygen, repeat the mantra: "Let in." As you prepare to exhale, imagine taking the flow of oxygen

and energy down through your entire body, passing through your lungs, moving down through your core abdominal area, flowing through your legs, and extending out through the tips of your toes. Try to visualize this energy releasing from your feet back into the environment as you say to yourself, "Let go."

3. With each inhale, imagine bringing in the flow of energizing oxygen up to your head and nourishing your busy brain as you repeat silently to yourself, "Let in." Then envision flushing the new energy through your entire body as you release the oxygen, along with any physical tension you might feel. Allow the energy to flow downward through your body, bringing with it a sense of complete relaxation as you repeat to yourself, "Let go." Imagine the energy pouring out the tips of your toes with a sense of release and relief.

4. Sometimes it's easy to become so focused on giving our energy to the people and things that matter to us that we forget to bring energy back into our system. As you breathe in this healing oxygen, you may want to think about other areas in your life in which you are blocking the good energy from soaking into your being; it might be from positive experiences in your life or from people who care about you and want to show you compassion and affection. Allow yourself to breathe in these feelings of loving support from the world around you so that with each exhale that you offer back out the world, you return an even greater, deeper sense of appreciation and gratitude.

5. With each flow of oxygen and energy moving into your body, extending up to your brain, and flushing through your entire being, appreciate and embrace this moment for what it is: energizing rhythm.

6. Continue your mantra, "Let in, let go," for a few moments. When you feel ready, gently open your eyes and return to your day, taking with you restored confidence in the renewed energy you now bring to the world around you.

Reprogram Your Operating System

You need to learn how to select your thoughts the way you select your clothes in the morning.

—Elizabeth Gilbert, *Eat, Pray, Love*

7

Step 4: Rethink

Our mind has the incredible power to change how we think, which has an immediate impact on how we feel. Research has shown that simply adjusting our mindset can have significant effects on objective, measurable outcomes, such as levels of hormone secretion, reduced pain, improved hearing, and decreases in body fat percentage. You've probably heard of the placebo effect before, often used negatively to describe things that don't work. However, the placebo effect has an effect, which means it does work; it has the power to trigger a significant change in the brain and body because we think it will work.

In fact, research has shown that inactive pills—the placebo—show benefits in 60 to 90 percent of diseases.[1] This includes both diseases with subjective endpoints, like anxiety or depression, and diseases with measurable physical changes, like osteoarthritis and cancer. Placebo treatments trigger complex neurobiological phenomena, including the activation of distinct brain areas, as well as peripheral physiology and the immune system. Alia Crum, a top Columbia Business School mindset researcher, calls the placebo effect "an incredible and consistent demonstration of the power of mindset to recruit healing properties in the body, even without active drug."

This phenomenon has been shown to have serious implications not just in pharmaceuticals but in medical procedures as well. In one study, researchers enrolled patients who were scheduled for reconstructive knee surgery. They went through all of the typical operating room steps, including undergoing anesthesia and having their knees cut open. But instead of having surgery, the doctors simply waited the time the surgery normally takes, sutured the patients back up, and monitored the results. Compared with before the surgery, these "sham-procedure" patients felt less pain, used less morphine, had more mobility, could climb more stairs, and had reductions in the objective amounts of swelling—all because they believed they'd had reconstructive surgery.[2]

New studies in neuroplasticity show that we have more control over how we think than we once knew. Although it's been long assumed that the brain is hardwired from a young age, advances in medical technology have provided us with a way to see the brain in action. Researchers can now analyze activity changes that occur in the brain as a result of shifts in thought patterns— and can even determine how new mental maps are forming because of repeated cognitive training.

The Power of Positivity

One of the best-researched areas of brain training is optimism and positivity—likely because a positive brain performs better on nearly all functions of cognitive ability than a neutral or negative one. As Shawn Achor describes in his book *The Happiness Advantage*, we've been sold a bill of lies when it comes to work success and happiness.[3] We assume that if we work hard and become successful, then we will be happy. But as studies on lottery winners and professional superstars reveal, if we're not happy before we get there and suddenly realize that improved status didn't help boost our spirits, we may end up feeling worse in the long run. The equation should read, "Be happy and work hard, and then you will be successful," not the other way around.

It turns out that people in a positive mood have many advantages over those who are negative or neutral, including mental flexibility. According to positive psychology researcher Sonja Lyobomirsky, author of the book *The How of Happiness*, "People in a positive mood are more likely to have richer associations with existing knowledge structures (things we already have committed to memory) and thus are more likely to be more flexible and original."[4] Martin Seligman, often called the godfather of the positive psychology movement, believes that positive people are more resilient because they are able to perform better—and are even stronger physically—when difficulties strike.[5]

Barbara Fredrickson of the University of North Carolina and author of the book *Positivity* has studied the power of positivity in companies with which she has researched and consulted. Fredrickson and her team analyze the words that employees say in business meetings to determine their "positivity ratio"—the ratio of positive to negative statements. According to Fredrickson, companies with a positivity ratio higher than 2.9 : 1 (or 2.9 positive statements for every negative statement) are flourishing. Organizations that fall below that ratio don't seem to be doing well economically. However, Fredrickson warns us not to go overboard with compliments, because anything above 13 : 1 may cause us to lose our credibility.[6]

Relationship expert John Gottman looked at a positivity ratio in conversations between married couples. He found that in relationships, a 2.9 : 1 ratio of positive-to-negative statements is not enough to make a partnership flourish. To reach that goal, couples need a 5 : 1 ratio of positive to negative—or five positive statements for every one critical statement. Gottman suggests that a 2.9 : 1 ratio means the couple is headed for divorce and a habit of 1 : 3 is an "unmitigated catastrophe."[7]

Mindset Matters

Mindset author Carol Dweck separates mindsets into two fundamental categories: growth and fixed.[8] People who believe that intelligence is a fixed trait—that is, you have it or you don't—have a fixed mindset. These individuals tend to believe that success is based on talent and may be quick to dismiss effort and hard work as something for the weak or less intelligent.

People who operate according to a fixed mindset often opt for easier tasks that require less effort, and they may give up quickly. Whether it's work related or involves an important relationship, these individuals often throw in the towel faster than people who believe they have the ability to work hard for change.

People with a growth mindset see difficulties as opportunities for growth. They're more willing to take risks, put in extra effort without feeling stupid, and recognize the benefit of learning, regardless of outcome. They believe they can develop their brains, abilities, and talents. In her research, Dweck found that individuals trained on a growth mindset pursue goals related to learning, not just outcomes or performance.

Multiple studies have shown that a growth mindset is beneficial in business. Negotiators who see things this way are more able and apt to push past obstacles to reach a mutually beneficial agreement. Business school students who were taught a growth mindset learned more skills and received better grades in their negotiation class. Leaders may benefit from a growth mindset because they are better equipped to coach and develop their employees and are quicker to notice improvement in their team than are leaders with a fixed mindset.

Having an optimistic or positive mindset has serious benefits, both in and out of the office. Studies show that a positive mindset has a significant impact on cognitive functioning in areas such as attention, intuition, and creativity. Being positive helps speed recovery from cardiovascular problems, lowers cortisol, reduces the inflammatory effect of stress, and improves the chance of living a long, healthy life. According to multiple studies, positive affect also produces future health and well-being.[9]

Although our mindset tendencies may be hardwired, the good news is that recent neuroscience research has demonstrated that the brain is more malleable and adaptable than we once thought. By using simple cognitive training exercises, similar to the ones we discussed in the previous chapters, we can rewire our mental maps to be stronger in areas that our genetic tendencies may have made weak. Like our muscles, our brain pathways weaken and start to atrophy if we don't use them regularly. This can be great when we want to decrease the power of negative habits, but it can undermine our goals when we lose strength in those areas that move us in a positive direction.

Rewire Your Patterns of Thought

Our brains contain trillions of neural connections that have cemented our habits of thought and behavior over time. Each time we have a thought, the brain fires chemicals that wire and rewire neural patterns. With repetition, these thoughts strengthen and become part of our automated system, which then conserves energy when we need to think or behave that way again. It can be frustrating when we've wired particular patterns of thought or behavior that we wish to change, because we often slip back into bad habits despite our best intentions.

Most people go wrong in one of two ways when trying to create a behavior change: They don't have the energy necessary to make adaptations in the brain, or they don't invest the time required to solidify the changes. Recent studies have shown that it can take an average of 60 days to rewire a thought or behavior pattern—sometimes more and sometimes less, depending on the habit and the individual.[10]

We must keep in mind that any change requires energy; if we have an empty tank, our brain is going to shut down unnecessary spending in an effort to help us survive. We fight our biggest battles with ourselves during these low-energy times. Although we need to make good choices to have good energy, we also need energy to make those good choices. Because we need to invest energy to change brain patterns, we can only take on a little bit of change at a time. We gain motivation and momentum as we start to build up our energy reserves; at this point, we're recharged and better able to create sustainable change moving forward.

Let's walk through one example of how to rewire a negative thought pattern, and then you can try one of your own. I've developed a simple five-step process, or five As, for changing our internal dialogue, one message at a time:

1. *Aware:* Become aware of the negative thought that's holding you back.

2. *Acknowledge:* Recognize the purpose that the old thought served.

3. *Appreciate:* Feel gratitude for the role it has served in protecting you until now.

4. *Adapt:* Change the statement to one that works better.

5. *Allow:* Give yourself time to practice.

The first step, or A, in changing our patterns of thought is to become *aware* of our internal dialogue. Habits inevitably come with a story that supports them, so if we're struggling to change behavior, we must first look at the message we're telling ourselves that makes it okay to continue it. For example, we say we want to eat healthier but then clean our plate because we don't want to waste food or because we recognize there are children starving in other countries. The reality is that we're likely to receive more than we need if we aren't in control of our portion sizes—and eating too much is waste whether we carry it on our waistline or toss it in the wastebasket. Another common example is when we want to take more breaks in our day. But as the alarm sounds for our time-out, we quickly remind ourselves of how many things need to get done and keep pushing through without a pause. By recognizing these messages, we can determine whether they're true and moving us in the direction of our goals. If they aren't, we have the power to rewrite them once we are able to fully let them go.

Before changing our script, it's helpful to *acknowledge* the purpose that the old thought served in trying to do something helpful for us. Our CFO brain is constantly trying to protect us, and a faulty thought pattern is almost always rooted in self-preservation. Eating too much food or pushing through break time can seem like the best choice when we're overwhelmed or fearful of running out of steam. By recognizing the old thought pattern's purpose, we can modify our new thought to take over in a healthier, more productive way. We may even want to incorporate the message into our new thought, such as "I recognize my brain wants me to eat extra food because I feel tired, but what I really need right now is to get some fresh air and go for a walk to recharge."

Once we acknowledge what our prior belief was trying to do for us, we should try to *appreciate* that at its core, it was serving some sort of protective function. Remember the "frenemy" brain, and consider what might have been going on until now that would cause it to say these things or try to motivate these behaviors. It's the brain's job to protect us when we're in survival mode, so we should be sure to thank it occasionally. This decreases defensiveness and resistance to the new message; after all, everyone wants to feel appreciated it for what they're trying to do, even if it's not working out the way they'd hoped. Each time we have a thought or behavior that seems to be pulling us away from our goals, we should try to see the situation from the brain's protective perspective. We might gain more understanding and find the negative pattern easier to rewire.

Based on what we're trying to accomplish, we can now *adapt* the message to one that better serves us. If we need energy, what are some healthier ways to recharge? If we feel overwhelmed by our to-do list, how can we convince ourselves that taking a break is critical to getting it all done?

The final step, or A, to rewire our thought process is often the toughest—that is, to *allow* adequate time for the changes to take hold. First, we think about one limiting belief that gets in the way of better energy management and practice going through the four initial steps outlined earlier to rewrite our story. Then, we commit to spending at least 3 to 5 minutes each day working through the new thought process. A recharge or movement break might be a great time to do some mental cross-training and practice while enhancing the circulation of glucose and oxygen to the brain.

Take a moment to walk through the following five As exercise. Focus on rewiring your thought process around one specific limiting belief that prevents you from taking the time and energy you need to recharge your energy throughout the day.

1. *Aware:* What is the negative thought that's holding you back? When you say to yourself, "I know I need to take time for myself during the day to recharge . . ." what *but* follows? "I know I need to take time for myself during the day to recharge, *but . . .*"

2. *Acknowledge:* What purpose did the old belief serve? Why would your brain fire a thought like that? What is it trying to protect? Are you trying to save time or energy, attempting to get more done in less time, or feeling too tired to spend energy on changing a habit that seems to be serving you?

3. *Appreciate:* Take a moment to feel gratitude for the role the old thought has served in protecting you. Until this point, you might not have been ready or able to make this change; your previous habits of thought kept you secure and gave you what you needed at that time. With appreciation for yourself, you can now move on to a new thought that supports a new behavior that will lead you closer to your goals.

4. *Adapt:* How can you change the statement to one that works better, considering your desire to take time for yourself during the day to recharge your energy? What do you need to hear yourself say to buy into this new way of taking care of yourself so that ultimately you are better able to take care of other people in your life? What message will motivate you to take action toward your new habits of oscillation during the day? Examples might be, "I need to put my oxygen mask on first so that I can take care of others," "Taking care of my body is business relevant," or "I need a calm, quiet mind and an energized body to accomplish my goals." Whatever the new message is, make sure that it sounds like something you would say and believe (not just what someone else wants you to believe) and that it inspires you to take action.

5. *Allow:* Give yourself adequate time and energy to practice your new thought pattern. Select a time in your schedule for it each morning so that you remember to go through the exercise. Keep in mind that it may take a week, a month, or a year to change one habit of thought, depending on how long the old message has been working for you and how deeply ingrained it has become. Be patient with yourself; ideally, you want to practice this new thought multiple times throughout the day as you start to integrate new supportive rituals into your daily routine.

What's Love Got to Do with It?

People often tell me that they wish they could have a job that allows them to follow their heart and do something truly meaningful. The great thing about a passionate career path is that the force of energy you're able to channel into your work is of the greatest intensity—because it brings such a laser focus on your priorities. The challenge: If you think it's tough to say no to work you don't like, try saying no when open doors hold opportunities you once believed would only be seen in dreams. How do you say no to something you'd pay good money to be able to do? In many ways, the things we love most cause us the most stress. After all, we wouldn't have such a strong emotional response if we didn't care.

Our stress dependence can become even greater when we love what we do, because (1) we feel grateful to work within our place of passion, (2) we feel bad complaining or even addressing our stress levels when we know other people have it "worse," or (3) we receive an even greater amount of neurochemical reward in the brain when we feel "in love" with what we're doing. It's hard enough to set limits on work when we have a boring job; it can feel nearly impossible when we feel inspired by what we do.

Although it can feel like we're floating along on cloud nine, even our greatest passions require extraordinary energy to sustain over time. Love, like life, requires healthy oscillation to keep it going. To bring our best self to the people and things we care about most—whether it be our friends, family, community, or career—we must build in time to rest, repair, and rebuild our energy regularly. Oftentimes, this requires that we think differently about what takes priority in any moment, whether it's turning our focus outward to serving our greatest missions in life or turning our attention inward to recharging and replenishing our energy. As we become more mindful of our ideal performance pulse during the day, we can continue to give the best of ourselves without feeling depleted or burning out.

As you become more aware of your thoughts and how they affect your behaviors, keep in mind that change requires energy. For your cognitive training to take hold and have a lasting impact on supporting your goals, you need to maintain your other practices of resting, repairing, and rebuilding your energy supply. This keeps your energy tank full, allowing your CFO brain to perceive abundance. Then it won't be stingy when it comes to sharing some of that energy for your internal work. The time and energy you spend now to rewire your patterns of thought will help support you in your stressaholic recovery process, strengthening your resilience and continuing to positively transform your relationship with stress.

The Rethink Checklist

- *Aware:* Become aware of the negative thought that's holding you back.
- *Acknowledge:* Recognize the purpose that the old thought served.
- *Appreciate:* Feel gratitude for the role it has served in protecting you until now.
- *Adapt:* Change the statement to one that works better.
- *Allow:* Give yourself time to practice.

Stepping Stone 4: Purpose, Perspective, and Positivity

Sometimes the best thing we can do to help balance the stress in our lives is to increase our scope of reference by looking at the bigger picture. Any shift away from the norm can feel like a threat when we're in survival mode, especially when our tank is empty. Knowing that the demands we face far exceed the energy we have in the moment can feel overwhelming, even though our challenges are temporary. One seemingly simple shift in the language we use to describe our current situation can trigger a dramatic change in our internal environment. It switches from a mode of fighting or running away from threats to being ready—even anticipating or being excited—to face challenges head on.

I remember an important lesson I learned early in my speaking career from a participant in one of my groups. He was an expert speaker who congratulated me on a job well done. I was surprised by the compliment and asked him if my nerves would ever go away. He warned me that I shouldn't wish away my nervous energy because it was one of the driving forces that gave me the edge I needed to get up on stage and perform to the audience. Without that energy, he said, the presentation might come across boring, stale, or lacking emotion. By simply shifting my interpretation of the energy I was feeling, I was suddenly able to use it for my benefit instead of letting it carry me into fears of another panic attack.

Although this knowledge was not enough for me to make a sudden leap into anxiety-free public speaking, it did help prepare me with techniques for seeing my engagements as an opportunity for growth. I began to recognize them as part of a challenging adventure that would cost extra energy to endure but would also lead me toward my most important goals of having a meaningful career, overcoming personal obstacles, and continuing to learn and grow through my experiences. Being able to build more resilience to the stress of public speaking has not only enabled me to see parts of the world I never imagined possible and build a flourishing career doing something I find fascinating; I'm also able to use my personal growth to help inspire and teach others who might be struggling with similar challenges. This adventure continues to be a blessing for me.

Shifting my internal dialogue from perceiving challenges as stresses to embracing them as adventures helps me prepare my mind and body to endure a bit more of an energy drain. When I recharge my energy regularly, I can use the experiences to continue to grow and become even more resilient. I invite you to try this practice when you are experiencing anxiety or stress to see whether it's helpful for you.

The simple mantra "Life is an adventure" can gently shift your brain into a more growth-based perspective. It prompts you to see the world around you as an opportunity to experience challenges that stimulate growth. When we recognize that we have what we need right in this moment, we allow the brain to disarm its protective guard. It's then ready to invite challenges and even temporary discomfort into our life to build our strength, improve our flexibility, and make us more resilient to future stress.

Try it now. Read the following instructions, and then walk through the steps on your own. You can also download a guided meditation track directing this practice at www.synergyprograms .com/stressaholic.

1. Get in a comfortable position and gently close your eyes.
2. Bring your awareness to the physical sensations of your breath as you inhale slowly and exhale calmly. With continued awareness on your physical body, bring the following mantra to mind: "Life is an adventure."
3. With each inhale, remind yourself that you have what you need in this moment, recognizing the security you can feel knowing you are providing your brain and body with precious oxygen for energy. As you exhale, allow your body to release any physical tension you might be experiencing, let

go of any thoughts about what you could or should be doing right now, and allow yourself to be in the moment.

4. Appreciate and embrace this moment for what it is: an adventure.
5. Continue your mantra, "Life is an adventure," for a few moments. When you feel ready, gently open your eyes and return to your day, taking with you restored confidence in the renewed energy you now bring to the world around you.

Here are other mantras you may want to try to help improve your mental flexibility, keep a positive perspective, and connect with your deeper sense of purpose:

"Get off the bench and get in the game."

"Let go, let God."

"Be still and know."

"Be here now."

"In this moment, all is well."

8

Step 5: Redesign

In this final step of our stressaholic recovery process, you will begin to redesign your lifestyle so that it supports your efforts to strategically manage your energy. A big part of this requires setting aside time when you can rest and invest energy back into your system. Merely knowing what to do has never been enough to cause sustainable change. You must have a strategic plan in which you feel confident—one that requires you to make a few small changes at a time to support the growth process. To do this, you start to create a pulse throughout the day by using consistent breaks to refuel energy through nutrition and movement and breaking up your workday into blocks that allow strategic engagement and disengagement.

Creating healthy oscillation requires that we identify rituals that can be implemented at both individual and organizational levels. The biggest problem with most current stress management programs is that they are reactive. In other words, companies use resources to make sure that people can get the help they need if something negative happens as a result of stress. Although this is an important safety net, only a very small percentage of employees use these types of services; oftentimes, significant damage has already been done. However, participants seem more apt to welcome proactive programs that build training and communication around a more global theme of building health and resilience. These initiatives also improve employee morale, because workers feel that their organization truly cares about their well-being. One example of this is a program offered by My Brain Solutions, in which resilience training is part of an overall physical and cognitive fitness training platform. This interactive solution typically see usage rates as high as 70 percent.[1]

Our conversation needs to move in the direction of a cultural shift that embraces not only healthy choices shown to significantly decrease health care costs to the organization but also to appropriate energy management strategies that keep employees fully focused and engaged and decrease the feeling of being overwhelmed, presenteeism (showing up physically but not being present mentally or emotionally), and burnout. It's time for organizations to start doing more than creating underutilized onsite workout facilities. Even resources like napping pods and recharge rooms are only great in theory if the corporate culture still suggests that anyone who uses them is lazy or weak. Successfully managing energy by encouraging employees to take consistent breaks is a sign of great strength. We all know how challenging it is to break away from the tight grasp of work, to-do lists, and deadlines to come back more fully fueled and prepared to work with greater intensity and sustainability as a result.

I can't tell you how often I talk to employees who confide in me that while they fully believe in and support the idea of energy management, they feel overwhelmed with the ceaseless demands placed upon them by leadership. If we wait to make changes to our personal routine until life makes it easier for us, then it's never going to happen. We must therefore take responsibility for doing the best we can despite our circumstances.

However, for us to create the big changes necessary for dramatic reductions in our shared stress addiction tendencies, we have to consider how we might work to shift the culture of organizations to one that supports individual efforts. We need to have more conversations about the way we're working and determine how we can optimize our energy for both performance and sustainable health, because both clearly affect the organization's productivity and long-term success.

When we look back on our previous steps, we know we need to design rituals that support a variety of changes. We know we must get adequate rest during the day, take recharge breaks that build in nutrition and movement, and complete strategic training that provides a healthy dose of stimulation to break down old physical and mental muscles before building them back up again to be stronger over time. To do this, we must establish a new way of setting boundaries and expectations so that we can take the time we need to practice, communicate with an effective attitude so that others know the intent behind our training, and allocate enough time to create a habit.

Let's start our focus on the part of the puzzle that you're most confident you can control: your personal routine. Keep in mind that your energy management starts from the moment you wake up in the morning and continues until you turn off the lights at night. Creating consistent rituals for basic self-care is essential to keeping your inner battery charged throughout the day.

Personal BEATs

It's important to recognize that many of our assumptions about the way we're supposed to be spending our energy—that is, that we should be going nonstop—are not grounded in truth. Many of our habits exist because we assume people have certain expectations of us or because that's the way everyone else seems to be working. Here's a favorite example: People often set an out-of-office message to respond to incoming e-mails when they're unavailable—usually on vacation, on a business trip, or even out sick. Typically it reads something like, "I will be out of the office on x-y-z dates with limited access to e-mail. If you need immediate attention, please contact thisotherperson@mycompany .com and he will be happy to assist you. Thank you." Now, when I send someone an e-mail and get that response, I always laugh to myself, wondering how long it will take to actually get a reply, knowing it's usually not long.

It happened to me this week. I received a wonderful out-of-office message from a guy I had been referred to for some website updates. I was hopeful that I wouldn't hear back from him until the time he returned, because his message said, "I am out of the country enjoying my honeymoon. I will not have access to e-mail, nor will I respond if I do (I am not interested in an early divorce). I will be back in the office on Thursday, August 29, and will address your e-mail as soon as possible. Thank you for your understanding and we will talk when I return." What a great message! It clearly set boundaries and expectations and used a dose of humor to share a positive attitude. I was so sure that I would not hear back for a couple of weeks that I was a bit discouraged when I received an e-mail from him early the next morning. I chalk it up to being a step toward progress, though because he sent the message and did so with fabulous intent.

The challenge comes when we don't do things like this and then hold to them consistently. Specifically, we fail to build up our distraction-resistance muscle that enables us the strength we need to truly disconnect when we want to.

The concept makes sense: If you tell people that you're not available, you can take the pressure off yourself to feel like you need to reply right away. But do you eliminate that pressure? Or are you so used to being constantly connected that you still check—just to make sure you're not missing anything? Do you tell yourself, "I'll respond quickly so that I don't have to deal with it later," convinced that you'll save yourself time, and stress, in the future? Why even take a vacation if you're not going to give yourself a break?

I know what you're thinking: You hate the idea of all that work piling up for you to deal with when you return. However, you've already determined that your system needs a break occasionally. So if you can't take a full week off and enjoy the downtime, what could you plan to do that would give your brain and body a chance to rest? Perhaps you'd be better off taking shorter vacations—where you actually take time away from work—more often. As with any recovery strategy, there is no one-size-fits-all approach. Some people feel better taking shorter breaks more often, like a long weekend each month; others need a more extended amount of time away to allow themselves adequate time to disconnect. The important thing is figuring out what you need and then developing and enacting the best action plan to make sure it happens.

The same thing applies when it comes to taking smaller recharge breaks throughout the day. Most people agree that we need to take better care of ourselves and oscillation seems like a healthy way to do that. However, it can feel almost impossible to pry ourselves from the tasks at hand when we're amid a chaotic work schedule. To have a plan we can stick with, it's critical that we first truly believe that what we're doing is important. We need a message or story that supports what we've practiced saying to ourselves. This is what keeps us motivated when facing challenges or sensing pressure from the outside to keep plugging away, despite plummeting energy levels. If this is still a challenge for you, I encourage you to reread the previous chapter walk through the rethink steps for creating a supportive story.

Once we have the right story in place, we can then set up the logistical process required to support our efforts. This includes clear *boundaries* and *expectations*, communicating with a positive *attitude*, and then allowing time for the new rituals or BEATs to become part of our automated routine. In doing so, we create a healthy rhythm that supports our energy replenishment strategies to keep our tank full, our brain out of conservation mode, and our system strong enough to be resilient to stress.

Boundaries

Decide what, where, and when you will set aside time for yourself to recharge throughout the day. Determine from the get-go that these time blocks are as important as any client meeting or appointment you've scheduled. Remind yourself that you're refueling your energy so that you can have more to give to the projects you need to complete, colleagues you partner with, and clients you serve. Also remember that recharging during the day increases the chance that you'll have energy left at the end of it. You'll be able to spend on time with friends, with family, or even on personal hobbies you once enjoyed or always wanted to try but were too tired or busy to do. Be as clear as possible on what, where, and when you will take your breaks and how you will communicate these breaks to other people who may want your attention during that time.

This last one can be a little tricky for an always-on professional environment. You might consider having a sign on your door or workspace that says "time out" or "recharging," putting an out-of-office message on your e-mail or voice mail temporarily, or blocking out time on your calendar in advance as if you were in a meeting—using whatever description you feel comfortable sharing. If you feel that your organization supports your right to take breaks, then schedule them in as such and allow yourself to be a great example of energy management for your coworkers. If you feel alone in your energy management journey, call it a client meeting. Alternatively, get in your car and go for a short drive, take a walk, or do something else that makes you physically unavailable; be sure that you're mentally and emotionally creating some temporary distance as well.

Expectations

You might be surprised to find out how supportive other people are of your recharge breaks when they know what to expect. It seems like we're all hyperaware of how responsive everyone else at our workplace is to e-mails and other communications, so we assume that we too must be available around the clock. Yet I have plenty of colleagues and clients who don't have this sense of urgency when it comes to responding. So I shifted my expectations once I learned that about them. I know I can expect to hear back from some people within the hour or at least a few hours. I quickly learned that others might take a couple of days, a week, or more to respond because of their schedule. But it's more than schedule. I've also realized that these slow responders tend to be those who block out time to respond when it works for them. They don't have their e-mail open constantly; they use their e-mail when they're ready.

When we're strategic about time and energy, we're better able to get things done quickly, effectively, and efficiently. We are more successful when we set aside time for particular tasks rather than reacting to whatever may pop up all day. Most of us intuitively know this. However, we feel pulled to the technological leash that keeps us feeling connected, needed, and available for exciting news that stimulates the brain. We must keep in mind that we are the ones who set and maintain expectations. Therefore, if we're always responding, people come to expect a quick response time. If you feel powerless to establish clear boundaries and manage expectations in a way that allows you this flexibility, you always have the ability to engage in clarifying conversations with others to find a middle ground that works for everyone involved.

Attitude

Communication is essential when it comes to establishing healthy boundaries and expectations. You want to be clear about your purpose and convey a positive and productive attitude about needing oscillation. This doesn't make you lazy or weak; rather, you're creating a healthy rhythm during the day that keeps your energy consistent and stable so that you can bring your best effort to your time investments. If people get the feeling that you're checking out or disengaged for some unknown reason, then you communicate a message of deprivation—which elicits a stress response in others. But if you use a constructive, fun, or humorous approach, you can share positive, abundant energy instead. Examples might be using language such as "I'm in airplane mode" when you're offline, using a door sign that states "recharging," or blocking off your shared calendar as "boosting brainpower" to let others know that you're temporarily off the grid. As long as you set boundaries and ensure that people know they'll have access to you when you're available, you're then able to give them your full and best energy in return for their patience.

Time

Setting up boundaries and expectations, even with the best of intentions and attitude, still takes time and consistency to become part of a daily routine. This new way of life will probably take a while to feel comfortable, so don't give up because it isn't coming easily. As I've said repeatedly throughout this book: Change requires an energy investment. It's even more challenging for your brain to feel secure in spending the energy you need to rewire thought and behavior habits when you're feeling overwhelmed. Research suggests that new habits take anywhere from 21 to 90 days to establish, so be patient with yourself and with others as you work to create your new routine. You may find it helpful to set several short-term goals to manage your expectations. Consider taking one week at a time. Pick a day of the week, maybe Monday morning or Friday afternoon, to look at your upcoming schedule and plug in necessary breaks. The more consistently you approach planning and preparation, the easier the routine becomes. Eventually, you will figure out what time of day and which strategies are giving you the best opportunity to rest, repair, and rebuild your energy. Then you can create even more structured guidelines that start to be second nature to how you do business.

Sample Individual BEATs

- Create a routine of 50-minute work hours.
- Break up your day into 20-minute focus blocks for tasks.
- Schedule 3- to 5-minute recharge breaks every hour.
- Set an alarm or use an app such as Bloom by Mindbloom, GPS for the Soul, or My Calm Beat by My Brain Solutions that reminds you of break times (no hitting the snooze button).

- Take snack breaks midmorning and midafternoon to keep blood sugar stable.
- Take a walk or stretch break at least every 90 minutes.
- Get outside for fresh air and a quick walk around the block.
- Meet up with a coworker for a social break (no shop talk allowed).
- Turn communication devices off when not actively in use (computer monitor, e-mail alerts, cell phone, etc.).
- Watch a funny video on YouTube (check out www.synergyprograms.com/lol for some of our favorites).
- Read or listen to a short chapter of a book not related to work.
- Send a handwritten thank-you note to someone you appreciate.
- Write down three things you feel grateful for each morning.
- Journal about the best part of your day each evening.
- Talk with your family at dinner about each person's funniest moment.
- Use drive time as quiet time; no radio or phone.
- Use long lines and traffic lights for deep breathing practice.
- Do something creative that's not related to work.
- Get a massage or other spa service.
- Dance, play, and laugh.

Organizational BEATs

One of the best ways to support personal stress and energy management efforts is to create organizationwide initiatives that encourage and even reward these best practices. As companies increasingly recognize the high costs of unmanaged stress with regards to health care, disability, and disengagement in the workplace, leadership is required to implement systemic policy changes that support employee well-being in a proactive and holistic way. Just as wellness programs have become commonplace in the work environment, building a culture of stress and energy management that supports both physical and cognitive fitness is essential. It's necessary not only for talent acquisition and retention but also for protecting the investment companies have in their most valuable resource: human capital.

Many organizations have recognized this need and begun to create corporate cultures that support the self-care and oscillation techniques we've discussed throughout this book. For example, Volkswagen shuts down e-mail servers 30 minutes after employees finish their shifts in an effort to decrease constant and obsessive e-mail use. They then turn it back on 30 minutes before start time. The great thing about this policy is that it doesn't keep people from getting things done if they need to put together a message for someone; it hinders the delivery of the message so that the receiving party isn't expected to act on it until the next business day. Although this may seem a bit extreme, companywide policies such as this may be the only way to guarantee that employees don't feel like they must constantly check for what might need their attention outside of business hours.

E-mail has quickly replaced phone calls as the most convenient form of communication, because it's quick and to the point. Yet this "time saver" can often do the opposite. Employees find themselves spending ever more time filtering through the information to determine what requires a response, an action, or merely an unsubscribe. It's important to think about how we use e-mail to make sure that we're not wasting precious time and energy. We need to streamline the process as much as possible and avoid using electronic communications to evade interactions that would work better face to face. Simple rules such as keeping messages brief and to the point, using the subject line to convey the main topic and set a priority level, and limiting use of group e-mails and copy/reply all messages to when necessary can help improve e-mail etiquette.

In addition to making communication more effective, many organizations are creating resources to make recharge breaks more accessible to their employees, especially in places where quiet space is hard to find. The open-space environment that many offices use nowadays may seem to stimulate teamwork and invigorate overall energy levels; however, it can also make it feel nearly impossible for employees to get away for mindful reflection. One idea is to set up recharge rooms with comfortable chairs, relaxed lighting, and a quiet-zone policy to give people a space to sit and rest or recharge in peace. Although it's not nearly as common, some companies have napping pods available for employees to lie down and meditate or take a quick snooze. Hydraulic desks that rise to a standing position or treadmill desks that allow employees to walk at a slow pace to encourage movement are being used more frequently, especially for groups that have traditionally been required to sit for long periods. What if you can't afford the latest technology devices to lift you out of your seat? Try putting an old box on top of your desk from time to time for a free boost.

Clear and consistent signage can help communicate the message that taking care of yourself leads to taking care of business within the office environment. You can use this language in posters and artwork around the office, placards in meeting rooms that encourage people to stand frequently or to leave their cell phone at the door when in session, or words written on staircases that encourage physical activity, such as steps that say "walk this way" or "pathway to health."

Perhaps my favorite strategy—one that I encourage every organization to attempt to make part of their corporate culture—is to implement a 50-minute work hour policy across the board. Several professions, including mental health counselors and massage therapists, already have this time structure as a standard. They recognize that to have an appointment starting on the hour, they need to build in time to transition between patients or clients. I'll never understand how we expect people to be in meetings for 60 minutes back to back to back without allowing time to get from one to the next physically, let alone being able to mentally make the shift from one topic to the next. How many times have you been in a meeting with a client still thinking about the one that just left or drifting off to thoughts about something else coming up later in the day that you still need to prepare for?

By building in a routine of transition time between appointments, meetings, or even tasks, we allow ourselves to wrap up, recharge, and then prepare for what's ahead without constantly worrying about being late or unprepared. Even though this makes perfect sense intuitively, we still fight the battle of feeling like we're wasting time by giving only 50 minutes instead of 60 minutes. It's important that we constantly remind ourselves that the quality of our work and our ability to give our full and best attention is measured not by the time we give but by the energy we bring to the time we have.

Sample Organizational BEATs

- 50-minute work hours
- 20-minute focus blocks for tasks
- 3- to 5-minute recharge breaks every hour
- Alarm or music that sounds throughout the office at break times
- Signage that supports energy management practices
- Walking paths in stairwells, outside the building, or across the campus

- Standing or treadmill desks
- Standing or walking meetings internally or with clients
- Cordless headsets available for all employees so they can stand or walk during calls
- Healthy food options in vending machines, in dining areas, and during meetings
- Recharge room with a quiet, comfortable space for individual downtime
- Group meditation, deep breathing, or heart rate variability training
- Energy ambassadors in the organization to help spread the message
- Energy coaches on staff to help set goals and create accountability
- Energy management strategies discussed in performance reviews
- Agendas for meetings and conferences that include consistently used breaks
- Policies that limit time for electronic communications (not after 6:00 PM or before 6:00 AM, for example)
- Wellness programs that offer incentives employees care about for self-care practices
- Team or organizationwide community service projects during the workweek
- Mentoring relationships for collaboration and brainstorming across departments

In an ideal world, all organizations would embrace and adopt policies that empower employees to manage their energy more effectively. However, demands on our time and resources will continue to skyrocket, so it's critical that we don't wait for the change to happen. Vast amounts of research have proved the return on investment for personal energy management strategies; so we know we're moving in the right direction. Ultimately, it's up to individuals to take responsibility for their recharge process. By creating a successful routine for yourself and bringing better energy to the team, you are able to inspire others around you to follow suit. You win, the company wins, and we all become healthier, happier, more productive, and resilient as a result.

Stepping Stone 5: Creating Your Optimal Performance Pulse

Our ability to have a healthy relationship with stress is grounded in our dedication to and persistence with taking care of ourselves from the inside out. We must remain fully committed to putting our own oxygen mask on first so that we can obtain the fuel we need to serve others. Although the strategies of resting, repairing, and rebuilding our energy supply throughout the day are common sense, they can't become common practice unless we invest the time and energy required to train new habits.

Despite the many demands and distractions we all face, our most difficult battle often takes place within ourselves: the struggle to make self-care a top priority. It may feel selfish or self-indulgent to spend time doing things that enable us to fully relax, but this is a critical part of what should be healthy oscillation. Think about how we care for young children; we want only the best for them, from healthy foods to consistent physical activity and plenty of good sleep. If only we could treat ourselves like the precious child we once were, allowing that same depth of love, nurturing, and compassion. We might find that our energy tank can be filled up. It might even start to overflow, giving us what we need to then provide that same love, nurturing, and compassion to the world around us. We should be able to serve others from the overflow of our cup, not from the mere droplets that seem to be left when we're exhausted and dying of thirst.

With this aim in mind, I provide a final stepping stone as a way to turn your affection, intention, and attention toward self-appreciation. Let's spend a few moments thinking about all of the hard work that your brain and body do to serve you throughout the day and give thanks.

Try it now. Read the following instructions, and then walk through the steps on your own. You can also download a guided meditation track directing this practice at www.synergyprograms .com/stressaholic.

1. Get in a comfortable position and gently close your eyes.

2. Bring your awareness to the physical sensations of your breath as you inhale slowly and exhale calmly. With continued awareness on your physical body, create your own mantra based on what you'd like to feel in this moment, starting with the words "I am." You might say, "I am peace," "I am happy," "I am healthy," "I am energized," or "I am love." Whatever it is that you wish to feel or be in this moment, declare that it is so as you continue to breathe and relax.

3. With each inhale, remind yourself that you have what you need, in this moment, recognizing the security you can feel knowing you are providing your brain and body with precious oxygen for energy. As you exhale, allow your body to release any physical tension you might be experiencing, let go of thoughts about what you could or should be doing right, and allow yourself to be in the moment.

4. Gently bring your attention to your physical body and the sensations of each inhale and exhale. Notice as your chest and belly expand and contract. On your next inhale, follow the path of your breath as it passes by your nostrils, and imagine it continuing through your nose and upward to your head as it fills you with energizing oxygen. As you gently exhale, imagine the breath passing from your head, through your

lungs, past your heart, and into your core abdominal area, washing down through your legs and out the tips of your toes as you fully release any tension and relax your body and your mind. Continue this cycle of moving energy in and up to the top of your head, and then releasing it down through your body and out the tips of your toes as you fully relax.

5. Place one hand on your heart, on your belly, or on the side of your face in whatever manner feels most soothing to you. Each of these positions can provide a sense of calm, similar to what a parent might do to quiet a fearful, sad, or insecure child. In this scenario, you are nurturing yourself with actions and thoughts that provide comfort and encourage stillness. By showing self-compassion, you express gratitude to yourself for all that you do and all that you are. The encouraging words *I am* help guide your thought process and aim your attention toward the positive, simultaneously offering the brain a chance to shift in that direction.

6. Spend a few minutes here, showing affection toward yourself with a comforting gesture and kind, encouraging words as you allow the feelings to soak into your entire being. See whether you can notice a subtle shift in your body chemistry as you start to regain homeostasis and balance, your body's natural way of being in a healthy rhythm of effort and ease. Continue to stay aware of your smooth, rhythmic breaths as you allow the energy of gratitude to flow from your fingertips inward toward your heart, belly, or face, showing yourself compassion for all that you do and, more important, all that you are. Allow yourself 1 or 2 minutes to simply reflect and let your body fill with a sense of self-appreciation.

7. Continue your mantra, "I am," for a few moments. When you feel ready, gently open your eyes and return to your day, taking with you restored confidence in the renewed energy you now bring to the world around you.

Here are other mantras you may want to try to help improve your mental flexibility, keep a positive perspective, and connect with your deeper sense of purpose:

"I am grateful."
"I am passionate."
"I am playful."
"I am adventurous."
"I am brave."
"I am committed."
"I am determined."
"I am authentic."
"I am worthy."
"I am enough."

Final Thoughts

I've often said we teach what we most need to learn, and that could not have been truer than when I set out to write this book. I'd just experienced a life-changing realization that a combination of my genetic makeup and lifestyle choices had made me addicted to stress at a cellular and chemical level. So I did what any good stress addict would do: I decided to write a book about it. There's no better way to provide ample access to my drug of choice than attempting to write a book.

My first thought was to create an oscillation process similar to what I've been discussing throughout this book. Instead of trying to write while I work, as I've done in the past, I would set aside ample time to focus solely on writing. I was committed to being fully engaged in the task at hand and being able to bring it my best energy. So I worked out my book tour to give me a full six weeks of committed time to the writing process. That is, until an opportunity to work with a new client came up—and with it more speaking engagements and more time on the road. How could I say no when the client was paying me good money to speak to a great audience and continue to share a message I was passionate about? Remember what I said in Chapter 7: Having a job you're passionate about is a blessing, but you have to work even harder to set good boundaries for rest and recovery. It's something I've repeatedly proved to myself.

So my writing sabbatical quickly filled up; however, I convinced myself that I'd still have time to write when I was on the road and even repeated the story that there is nothing like work to keep me from having a meltdown when I'm stuck on a plane during turbulence. Like numbing out with any other drug, work stress gives your brain something more urgent to focus on than being 30,000 feet in the air. The problem wasn't my lack of time, however; it was my lack of energy. As I'm sure many of you know, travel is a brain drain. Time zone changes, dry air, forced sitting for long periods, missed flights, weather patterns, germs galore, and tired, irritable people make for an energy management challenge of the highest degree. Even though I know how to make healthy choices, when you're running on empty, it's nearly impossible to opt for the salad when there is a buttery pretzel roll or unlimited glasses of wine available to soothe your weary soul.

Despite my best intentions, the travel and the stress caught up with me again—and again, my brain and body began to break down, spiking my anxiety levels and terrorizing me with fear that I'd taken on too much. Writing a book about stress addiction while facing my own addiction head on seemed to be hitting too close to home. I found myself wishing I had guidance for how to calm the craziness spinning in my mind. Then I realized that it was right in front of me. I knew what to do; heck, I was writing a book about it. I went back to Chapter 1 and reread my assessment of stress addiction and how serious of a concern it is to all of us. I found myself nodding to my words as I described our serious stress problem and then skimmed through my ideas for how to use stress for success.

Then I followed my five-step process to again try to break free from unnecessary sources of stress, both internally and externally. I even booked myself a stay at a retreat in Mexico for a few days to get away from the city noise and construction that was keeping me up at night and distracting me during the day. I realize not everyone can escape to Mexico when they need a break, but I believed my book—and my sanity—depended on it. Although it was a financial investment that I hadn't expected, I thought of all the other expenses I incur regularly—from work to personal, from business trips to doctor visits. This recognition challenged my thinking about whether spending time and money on my self-care was worth it. Of course it was; I would easily pay twice that much for a marketing person to help me spread the word about the book or for a Web developer to give me a great website. Why do we think so long and hard (and usually talk ourselves out of it) when it comes to investing that same time and money on our most valuable resource—our own energy?

I share this story with you for two reasons. First, I think it's important to continue to revisit our internal dialogue about how much it's worth to take care of ourselves. Our body is business relevant, because it is our vehicle to get through life. Yet most people check the oil in their car more frequently than they look at their blood work to see what's going on under their own hood. To be extraordinary at anything, whether it is at work or at home, as a leader in our organization or as a leader in our family or community, we must take care of ourselves first. We have to remember to put our oxygen mask on to help others. I hope you understand that, believe it, and start to create your own messages that support your ability to make more self-compassionate and energizing choices. You must be responsible for the energy you bring to the world, and by bringing more of yourself, you empower others to do the same, creating a significant ripple effect for the better.

Second, I want you to know that like any other addiction, recovery from stress is a lifelong process. You don't take a few steps and then find yourself at the finish line, where you can kick back and watch everyone else race. This is just part one of the journey. Rather than looking at life as a marathon in which we continually move forward toward our goal and conserve energy so that we can make it for the long haul, imagine it as a series of shorter sprints. A sprinter mentality gives you a clear view of the finish line. Sprinters are able to give everything they've got for a short period to maximize their effort, knowing that recovery time will happen at the end. Once they've recovered, sprinters can again take their mark at the starting gate with their eyes on the prize for the next race and give their full energy to get there as quickly and efficiently as possible.

You're going to make mistakes. False starts happen, and we trip from time to time; but that's all part of the journey. Making mistakes is the only way for deep learning to occur. When we stumble or face obstacles, we must figure out a solution or course correction. We'd never have the stimulation we need to grow or adapt if things were always easy. Like the stress in our lives, we need these obstacles to help us improve our technique and learn even better ways of reaching our most important goals.

In *Stressaholic*, I've provided you with five steps that I believe will help you transform your relationship with stress. But remember: It isn't something you do once and then forget about. I hope you will commit these steps to memory and walk through them again when you face challenges or feel overwhelmed, like I have learned to do each time I face my fears. Ask yourself:

- Am I getting the rest I need? If not, how will I build it into my routine? What will I do, when, and where?

- Am I providing my brain and body with a chance to repair regularly by fueling my system with good nutrients, like healthy food and frequent movement? Am I getting enough sleep? If not, how will I build it into my routine? What will I do, when, and where?

- Am I challenging myself to grow in areas that I need to maintain to be fit and have greater energy? Do I push myself physically every few days with some sort of interval training? Do I engage in mentally stimulating activities and conversations? If not, how will I build it into my routine? What will I do, when, and where?

- Am I able to see positive outcomes of stress in my life? Do I take time to count my blessings and enjoy present-moment gratitude? Am I telling myself a harmful story that's keeping me stuck in negative habits? If so, walk through the five As of the rethink process (given in Chapter 7) to provide yourself with a better message to support healthy choices.

- Do I consistently engage in my supportive rituals? Do I set clear boundaries and expectations, communicate with a positive attitude, and allow time for these strategies to become habits—in other words, do I create life BEATs to provide oscillation in my daily routine? If not, try creating one BEAT right now to create that time and space to recharge regularly.

Like any relationship in our life, our relationship with stress is one that will always require us to invest time and energy to keep it healthy. Trust that you have everything you need to create a healthy relationship, remain aware of your symptoms of stress so that you can quickly respond as needed, and stay the course. As you see your health, energy, productivity, and performance begin to soar, your loved ones will thank you for it—and you will thank yourself.

Notes

Chapter 1: Are You a Stress Addict?

1. Cryer, B. (1996). *Neutralizing Workplace Stress: The Physiology of Human Performance and Organizational Effectiveness.* Presented at: Psychological Disabilities in the Workplace, The Centre for Professional Learning, Toronto, Canada, June 12, 1996.

2. Peele, S. (2012). The Meaning of Addiction Has Changed: Addiction Is Not a Characteristic of Things. Available at: www.huffingtonpost.com/stanton-peele/addiction_b_1874233.html

3. Selye, H. (1956). *The Stress of Life.* New York: McGraw-Hill.

4. Humphrey, J. (2005). *Anthology of Stress Revisited: Selected Works of James H. Humphrey.* Hauppauge, NY: Nova Science Publishers.

5. Sapolsky, R. (2004). *Why Zebras Don't Get Ulcers.* New York: Holt Paperbacks.

6. Epel, E., Blackburn, E., Lin, J., Dhabhar, F., Adler, N., Morrow, J., & Cawthon, R. (2004). Accelerated telomere shortening in response to life stress. *Proceedings of the National Academy of Science, 101*(49): 17312–17315. Available at: http://www.ncbi.nlm.nih.gov/pubmed/15574496/

7. Rosen, L. (2013). Phantom Pocket Vibration Syndrome: What does it tell us about our obsession with technology? *Psychology Today.* Available at: http://www.psychologytoday.com/blog/rewired-the-psychology-technology/201305/phantom-pocket-vibration-syndrome

8. American Psychiatric Association. (2000). *Diagnostic and Statistical Manual of Mental Disorders* (4th ed., text rev.). Arlington, VA: American Psychiatric Association. doi: 10.1176/appi.books.9780890423349

9. Felitti, V., Anda R., Nordenberg D, Williamson D., Spitz A., Edwards V., Koss M., & Marks J. (1998). Relationship of childhood abuse and household dysfunction to many of the leading causes of death in adults. The Adverse Childhood Experiences (ACE) Study. *American Journal of Preventative Medicine, 14*(4): 245–258.

Chapter 2: Why Taking It Easy Is Hard

1. Meyer, D. & Kieras, D. (1997a). A computational theory of executive cognitive processes and multiple-task performance: Part 1. Basic mechanisms. *Psychological Review, 104,* 3–65.

2. National Safety Council. (2010). *Understanding the Distracted Brain.* Available at: http://www.nsc.org/safety_road/Distracted_Driving/Documents/Dstrct_Drvng_White_Paper_Fnl%282%29.pdf

3. Thompson, C. (2005). "Meet the Life Hackers." *New York Times.* Available at: www.nytimes.com/2005/10/16/magazine/16guru.html

4. American Society of Addiction Medicine. (2011). *Definition of Addiction.* Available at: http://www.asam.org/for-the-public/definition-of-addiction

5. Rosch, P. J., ed. (2001, March). "The quandary of job stress compensation." *Health and Stress, 3,* 1–4.

6. American Institute of Stress. *Workplace Stress.* Available at: http://www.stress.org/americas-1-health-problem

7. Kessler, R., Chiu W., Demler, O., & Walters, E. (2005). Prevalence, severity, and comorbidity of twelve-month DSM-IV disorders in the National Comorbidity Survey Replication (NCS-R). *Archives of General Psychiatry, 62*(6): 617–27.

8. Kessler, R., Akiskal, H., Ames, M., Birnbaum, H., Greenberg, P., Hirschfeld, R., Jin, R., Merikangas, K., Simon, G., & Wang, P. (2006). Prevalence and effects of mood disorders on work performance in a nationally representative sample of U.S. workers. *American Journal of Psychiatry, 163,* 1561–1568.

9. Attitudes in the American Workplace Survey. Available at: http://americaninstituteofstress.org/wp-content/uploads/2011/08/2001Attitude-in-the-Workplace-Harris.pdf

10. Attitudes in the American Workplace Survey. Available at: http://americaninstituteofstress.org/wp-content/uploads/2011/08/2001Attitude-in-the-Workplace-Harris.pdf

11. The American Institute of Stress. Available at: http://www.stress.org/workplace-stress/

12. Ibid.

13. AOL. (2007). *Think you might be addicted to email? You're not alone. AOL's third annual "Email addiction" survey.* Available at: http://www.timewarner.com/newsroom/press-releases/2007/07/Think_You_Might_Be_Addicted_to_Email_Youre_Not_Alone_07–26–2007.php.

Chapter 4: Step 1: Rest

1. Holt-Lunstad, J., Smith, T., & Layton, J. (2010). Social Relationships and Mortality Risk: A Meta-analytic Review. *PLOS Medicine*, 7(7), 1–20.

2. Wilson, R., Krueger, K., Arnold, S., Schneider, J., Kelly, J., Barnes, L., Tang, Y., & Bennett, D. (2007). Loneliness and Risk of Alzheimer's Disease. *Archives of General Psychiatry*, *64*(2): 234–240. doi: 10.1001/archpsyc.64.2.234.

3. Siegel, D. (2010). *Mindsight: The New Science of Personal Transformation*. New York: Random House.

4. The Institute for Responsible Technology. Available at: http://www .responsibletechnology.org/gmo-basics/gmos-in-food

5. Patel, A.V., Bernstein, L., Deka, A., Feigelson, H.S., Campbell, P.T., Gapstur, S.M., Colditz, G.A., & Thun, M.J. (2010). Leisure time spent sitting in relation to total mortality in a prospective cohort of U.S. adults. *American Journal of Epidemiology*, *172*(4): 419–429.

6. National Institutes of Health. (2005). *Your Guide to Healthy Sleep*. Available at: http://www.nhlbi.nih.gov/health/public/sleep/healthy_sleep.pdf

7. Colten, H., & Altevogt, B., eds. (2006). Institute of Medicine (US) Committee on Sleep Medicine and Research. Washington, DC: National Academies Press. Available at: http://www.ncbi.nlm.nih.gov/books/NBK19961/

8. Debarnot, U. et al. (2011). Daytime naps improve motor imagery learning. *Cogn Affect Behav Neurosci. 11*(4): 541–50. doi: 10.3758/s13415–011–0052-z. Available at: http://www.ncbi.nlm.nih.gov/pubmed/21842279

9. Holt-Lunstad, J., Smith, T., & Layton, J. (2010). Social relationships and mortality risk: A meta-analytic review. *PLOS Medicine*, 7(7): 1–20.

10. Ybarra, O., Bernstein, E., Winkielman, P., Keller, M., Manis, M., Chan, E., & Rodriguez, J. (2008). Mental exercising through simple socializing: Social interaction promotes general cognitive functioning. *Personality and Social Psychology Bulletin*, *34*(2): 248–259.

11. Hawkley, L., et al. (2006). Loneliness is a unique predictor of age-related differences in systolic blood pressure. *Psychology and Aging*, *21*(1), 152–164.

Chapter 5: Step 2: Repair

1. Achor, S. (2012). Positive Intelligence. *Harvard Business Review*. Retrieved from http://hbr.org/2012/01/positive-intelligence

2. Seligman, M., Steen, T.A., Park, N., & Peterson, C. (2005). Positive psychology progress: Empirical validation of interventions. *American Psychologist, 60*(5): 410–421.

3. Scarmeas, N. (2009 August) Physical activity, diet, and risk of Alzheimer's disease. *JAMA Psychiatry, 302*(6), 627–637. Available at: http://www.ncbi .nlm.nih.gov/pubmed/19671904

4. Paoletti, R., Poli, A., Conti, A., & Visioli, F., eds. (2012). *Chocolate and Health*. Springer: Milan, Italy.

5. Donaldson, M. (2004). Nutrition and cancer: A review of the evidence for an anti-cancer diet. *Nutrition Journal, 3*(19). DOI: 10.1186/1475–2891–3– 19. Available at: http://www.nutritionj.com/content/3/1/19

6. Society for Neuroscience (2003). Diet may improve cognition, slow aging, and help protect against cosmic radiation. *ScienceDaily*. Available at: http://www.sciencedaily.com/releases/2003/11/031110054644.htm

7. Kris-Etherton, P., Harris, W., & Appel, L. (2003). Fish consumption, fish oil, omega-3 fatty acids, and cardiovascular disease. *Circulation, 106*(21): 2747–57.

8. Assuncao M., et al. (2009). Effects of dietary coconut oil on the biochemical and anthropometric profiles of women presenting abdominal obesity. *Lipids. 44*(7): 593–601.

9. National Center for Health Statistics. Health, United States, 2012: With Special Feature on Emergency Care. Hyattsville, MD. 2013.

10. Prochaska, J., Norcross, J., & DiClemente, C. (2007). *Changing for Good: A Revolutionary Six-stage Program for Overcoming Bad Habits and Moving Your Life Positively Forward*. New York: William Morrow.

11. Hayward, R., & Lien, C. (2011). Echocardiographic evaluation of cardiac structure and function during exercise training in the developing Sprague–Dawley rat. *Journal of the American Association for Laboratory Animal Science, 50*(4): 454–461. Available at: http://www.ncbi.nlm .nih.gov/pmc/articles/PMC3148638/#__ffn_sectitle.

12. The American Heart Association Recommendations for Physical Activity in Adults, (2013). Available at: http://www.heart.org/HEARTORG/ GettingHealthy/PhysicalActivity/StartWalking/American-Heart-Association-Guidelines_UCM_307976_Article.jsp

13. The American College of Sports Medicine, (2011). Quantity and quality of exercise for developing and maintaining cardiorespiratory, musculoskeletal, and neuromotor fitness in apparently healthy adults: Guidance for prescribing exercise. *Medicine & Science in Sports & Exercise, 43*(7), 1334– 1359. Available at: http://journals.lww.com/acsm-msse/Fulltext/2011/ 07000/Quantity_and_Quality_of_Exercise_for_Developing.26.aspx

14. Laughter Yoga International. General Article on Laughter Yoga: An Overview. Available at: http://www.laughteryoga.org/english/news/news_details/405

15. Brian, M. (2000). How Laughter Works. Available at: http://science.howstuffworks.com/life/laughter.htm

Chapter 6: Step 3: Rebuild

1. McCraty, R., & Tomasino, D. *Heart Rhythm Coherence Feedback: A New Tool for Stress Reduction, Rehabilitation, and Performance Enhancement.* Boulder Creek, CA: HeartMath Research Center, Institute of HeartMath. Available at: http://www.macquarieinstitute.com/health/professional/hrv_biofeedback.pdf

2. Loehr J. & Schwartz T. (2003). *The Power of Full Engagement: Managing Energy, Not Time, Is the Key to High Performance and Personal Renewal.* New York, NY: Free Press (Division of Simon & Schuster).

3. The American College of Sports Medicine. (2011). Quantity and quality of exercise for developing and maintaining cardiorespiratory, musculoskeletal, and neuromotor fitness in apparently healthy adults: Guidance for prescribing exercise. *Medicine & Science in Sports & Exercise, 43*(7), 1334–1359. Available at: http://journals.lww.com/acsm-msse/Fulltext/2011/07000/Quantity_ and_Quality_of_Exercise_for_Developing.26.aspx

4. Klika, B., & Jordan, C. (2013). High-intensity circuit training using body weight for maximum results with minimal investment. *ACSM's Health and Fitness Journal, 17*(3), 8–13. Available at: http://journals.lww.com/acsm-healthfitness/Fulltext/2013/05000/HIGH_INTENSITY_CIRCUIT_TRAINING_USING_BODY_WEIGHT_.5.aspx?WT.mc_id= IIPxADx20100319xMP

5. Kaminsky, L., Padjen, S., and LaHam-Saeger, J. (1990). Effect of split exercise sessions on excess post-exercise oxygen consumption. *British Journal of Sports Medicine, 24*(2), 95–8. Available at: http://www.ncbi.nlm.nih.gov/pubmed/2265322

Chapter 7: Step 4: Rethink

1. Benson, H., & Friedman, R. (1996). Harnessing the power of the placebo effect and renaming it "remembered wellness." *Annual Review of Medicine, 47*, 193–9. Available at: http://www.ncbi.nlm.nih.gov/pubmed/8712773

2. Moseley, J., et al. (2002). A controlled trial of arthroscopic surgery for osteoarthritis of the knee. *New England Journal of Medicine*, *347*(2), 81–8. Available at: http://www.ncbi.nlm.nih.gov/pubmed/12110735

3. Achor, S. (2010). *The Happiness Advantage: The Seven Principles of Positive Psychology That Fuel Success and Performance at Work*. New York: Random House.

4. Lyubomirsky, S. (2008). *The How of Happiness: A New Approach to Getting the Life You Want*. New York: The Penguin Press.

5. Seligman, M.E.P. (2002). *Authentic Happiness: Using the New Positive Psychology to Realize Your Potential for Lasting Fulfillment*. New York: Free Press.

6. Fredrickson, B. (2009). *Positivity: Top-Notch Research Reveals the 3 to 1 Ratio That Will Change Your Life*. New York: Random House.

7. The Gottman Institute. Research FAQs. Available at: http://www .gottman.com/research/research-faqs/

8. Dweck, C. (2006) *Mindset: The New Psychology of Success*. New York: Random House.

9. Fredrickson, B., & Losada, M. (2005). Positive affect and the complex dynamics of human flourishing. *The American Psychologist*, *60*(7), 678–86. Available at: http://www.ncbi.nlm.nih.gov/pmc/articles/PMC312 6111/.

10. Lally, P., van Jaarsveld, C., Potts, H., & Wardle, J. (2010). How are habits formed: Modelling habit formation in the real world. *European Journal of Social Psychology*, *40*(6), 998–1009.

Chapter 8: Step 5: Redesign

1. My Brain Solutions. Available at: https://www.mybrainsolutions.com/ Pages/employers.aspx

Resources

Websites

For free brain training exercises and guided relaxation audio tracks, visit www.synergyprograms.com/braingym.

For audio tracks and exercises specific to this book, visit www.synergyprograms.com/stressaholic.

For more information on stress management, including current stress statistics, visit the American Institute of Stress at www.stress.org.

Books

Brain Plasticity and Brain Training

- *Brain Rules*, John Medina
- *Buddha's Brain*, Rick Hanson
- *Imagine*, Jonah Lehrer
- *Mindset*, Carol Dweck
- *Mindsight*, Daniel Siegel
- *Positivity*, Barbara Fredrickson
- *Rapt*, Winifred Gallagher
- *The Happiness Advantage*, Shawn Achor
- *The How of Happiness*, Sonja Lyubomirsky
- *The Talent Code*, Daniel Coyle
- *Think Smart*, Richard Restak
- *Willpower*, Roy Baumeister and John Tierney

Healthy Aging

- *Counterclockwise*, Ellen Langer
- *Flourish*, Martin Seligman
- *The Blue Zones*, Dan Buettner
- *Younger Next Year*, Chris Crowley and Henry Lodge

Nutrition

- *Eat to Live*, Joel Fuhrman
- *In Defense of Food*, Michael Pollan
- *Mindless Eating*, Brian Wansink
- *The Beck Diet Solution*, Judith Beck
- *The End of Overeating*, David Kessler

Physical Activity and Exercise

- *SPARK: The Revolutionary New Science of Exercise and the Brain*, John Ratey

Stress Management

- *Getting Things Done*, David Allen
- *The Relaxation Response*, Herbert Benson
- *Why Zebras Don't Get Ulcers*, Robert Sapolsky

Sleep

- *Power Sleep*, James Maas

Social Connection

- *Loneliness*, John Cacioppo and William Patrick

Purpose and Storytelling

- *Believe Me*, Michael Margolis
- *The Power of Full Engagement*, Jim Loehr and Tony Schwartz
- *The Power of Purpose*, Richard Leider
- *The Power of Story*, Jim Loehr

Index

Note: Page reference in italics refer to figures.